To Paul.

Hope you enjoy the read

In the Name
of the Son

all the best

Declan Duggan

Declan Duggan

Published by Filament Publishing Ltd
16, Croydon Road, Waddon,
Croydon, Surrey, CR0 4PA UK
Telephone +44 (0)20 8688 2598
Fax +44 (0)20 7183 7186
info@filamentpublishing.com
www.filamentpublishing.com

© Declan Duggan 2012

Printed by Berforts Group - Stevenage and Hastings
Distributed by Gardners

ISBN 978-1-908691-36-1

The right of Declan Duggan to be identified as the author
of this work has been asserted by him in accordance with
the Designs and Copyright Act 1988

Dedication

We all deal with grief in our own different way. When we lose a parent (and I can speak on a personal level having lost both of mine), somehow you are able to deal with that loss. Our human and psychological make-up allows us to accept death in the natural order, that our parents go before we do.

These are the very people that we have known since birth and that we have grown up with and loved, laughed and cried with. This is a type of loss that, although still very hard to take and you remain sad for a long time, our own body and mind allows us to deal with (and manage) our grief in a healing sort of way.

We as a family of 11 brothers (sons) and one sister (daughter) deal with our grief and loss both individually and as a family. We relive all the good times that we had growing up in Dublin and in Luton, taking turns in story telling of all the funny things and not so funny things that happened to us all.

There are times that we laugh until we cry remembering all the good times and especially the stories surrounding our dad. He was a naturally funny and an accident-prone person, but with great sense of humour; we were all lucky that this gene was passed down to all of us.

There is nothing in the way that we are made that prepares us for the loss of a child. There is nothing in our mind, body or soul that helps us cope with a tragedy such as this. I still to this day can't offer or come up with any reasonable explanation or describe in any way how a parent can get over losing a child.

I have come to terms with the fact that I will have to live with the unbearable pain and profound loss until the end of my days on this earth.

My broken heart will only be repaired when we are both reunited in the next world.

This book is dedicated to all the families who have lost a loved one.

And to my mum and dad, Lena and Bill.

Bill and Lena Duggan on their
wedding day

Acknowledgements

There have been many people that have helped me on my journey these past 15 years or so, and for that I am eternally grateful.

I would like to especially thank the following: Margaret Moran; Gwyneth Dunwoody; Mo Mowlam; Gill Harris; Margaret Beckett, MP; Lisa Peddar; Lisa Roe; Kate Robbins; Charles Clarke; David Blunkett, MP; Lord Bill McKenzie; Nigel Wright; Paul Burrell; Peter Deighan; John Clifford; Danny McIroy; Stuart Bassett; Ian Fletcher; Graham Keeble; Julian Peek; Jim Nicol; Carl Newbury; Dave and Sally Collins; Jim Davey; Larry Cooney; Jim Carwey; Neil Rioch; Jay Saklani; Brendon Sherry; Marco Amitrano; Humphrey Deegan; Andy and Lisa Lomas; Dave Mathews; Shay and John McAuley; Phil Crace; Ken Moodie; Ken Brown; Sandy Jones.

Thanks to Philip Maule (Phil the Suit).

Thanks also to my brothers and sister – too many to mention!

Thanks to my children, Kerrie, Roisin, Patrick, Danny and Sinead.

Thanks to someone who has had to put up and live with me while I've been on this journey of campaigning, raising money, fighting injustice, being away from home for so long – my darling wife Derry.

A special thanks to Dean M Drinkel for helping me write this book.

And to all those that I've missed but not mentioned (as there are just far too many names), this is a big thank you for all your help, generosity, love and support throughout my darkest years.

Declan Duggan

Contents

Foreword from David Blunkett MP

This book demonstrates how a personal tragedy can turn into a successful campaign to save the lives of others and, above all, to bring justice where previous practice and legislation denied it to loved ones and friends.

The tragedy which befell Declan Duggan's son Kevin and the impact on the family was made worse, as Declan spells out, by the inability of the criminal justice system to bring to book the individual responsible because of outdated laws.

The campaign of Declan, and his local Member of Parliament of the time, stimulated the interest and commitment of so many people who then joined in to make democracy work.

For that is what has been achieved here.

An individual with determination and commitment, driven by the desire for justice to be seen to be done, turned a local campaign into a demonstration of how such tenacity can create living monuments (such as The Kevin Duggan Golf Academy) together with how to change the world for the better.

When I became Home Secretary in June 2001, this campaign had already created the momentum that allowed me to use the Policy White Paper of December 2001 and then the Police Reform Act 2002 to change the law. Making sense of nonsense, allowing blood tests to be taken from those where it was suspected that alcohol or drugs had contributed to the behaviour of drivers and the subsequent tragedy to passengers and pedestrians alike.

I believe that the wider messages this book contains will both touch and inspire readers. I congratulate Declan on giving so much of his life to a commemoration of that of his son.

Rt. Hon. David Blunkett MP
Member of Parliament for Sheffield Brightside and Hillsborough

Declan Duggan

Foreword from Sandy Jones

I would imagine that many of you who are about to read this wonderful book may wonder why the Chief Executive of The Professional Golfers' Association would be involved in writing this foreword.

I first met Declan Duggan on 11th July 2002 at the opening of The Kevin Duggan Golf Academy, a facility that in the last decade has done so much to improve the lives of under-privileged and disadvantaged children within its community.

That moment when I met Declan was certainly one that was very inspirational in my own life. From the great tragedy he endured, much good has emerged.

The game of golf and its core values of honesty, integrity, respect, fair play and desire are central to this story.

Golf provided a sanctuary in the life of Declan Duggan when he needed it most and his story will provide inspiration to all who read this book.

Sandy Jones
Chief Executive
The Professional Golfers' Association

Foreword from Lord Bill McKenzie

As this books portrays, The Kevin Duggan Golf Academy was the brainchild of Declan who wanted his son's passion for golf to endure as an inspiration for future generations of young people, especially those from disadvantaged backgrounds.

Stockwood Park in Luton was the natural location for the Academy, and it was Declan's advocacy and commitment to the concept that won the support of Luton Borough Council which recognised its unique approach. Despite this support, there were still challenges to face; some local opposition to the use of this site, and funding to secure.

But the council kept the faith as did the Duggan family and their many friends and supporters. Kevin's legacy has now been delivered — spaces on the driving range, a new nine-hole course, dozens of young people introduced to a discipline and a competitive sport they might have thought not for them. A chance to dream of being the next Rory McIlroy or Tiger Woods.

A shining example to those entrusted with our Olympic legacy.

Lord Bill McKenzie
Former Leader, Luton Borough Council

Foreword from Kevin Whately

In the decade or so that we have been pals, it was soon after his son Kevin was killed in a car crash, Declan has successfully lobbied parliament to change the drink-drive laws. He raised hundreds of thousands of pounds to build a new golf academy including a nine-hole par three golf course, fought to improve community relations, brought up a family, put together a new forthcoming musical, and written this book… all while running the liveliest pub in the area. He is a 'Human Dynamo'; one of life's "CAN DOERS", especially in adversity, and truly a man of principal and loyalty.

I hope you will be exhilarated by his story.

Kevin Whately
Actor

Foreword from Ken Brown

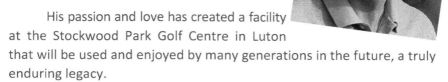

As soon as Declan approached me asking for my help in creating the Kevin Duggan Golf Academy, it was clear that I would be working with someone who's drive and enthusiasm was unrivalled.

His passion and love has created a facility at the Stockwood Park Golf Centre in Luton that will be used and enjoyed by many generations in the future, a truly enduring legacy.

Ken Brown

Former PGA, Ryder Cup and Scottish International

Now BBC Correspondent and golf commentator

Declan Duggan

Introduction

It was an old friend of mine, John Hughes (once from Luton but now living in Clonakilty, West Cork) who spread the word in Ireland about my campaign for justice, following the death of my 19-year-old son Kevin and my subsequent endeavour to get the drink-driving laws changed in the United Kingdom.

Whilst I was in Ireland for a family wedding in November 2009, I was contacted by John and a friend of his, Humphrey Deegan. Humphrey, also from Clonakilty, is a town councillor who represents Fine Gael[1]. He had been impressed by what had been achieved by our campaign team and he brought this to the attention of the Fine Gael leadership.

Fine Gael at that time was the opposition party in the Irish government. Enda Kenny[2] was the party leader and Fergus O'Dowd[3] was the opposition spokesman on transport affairs in the Dial.

Enda Kenny requested a meeting to hear for himself, the story of how an Irishman living in England took on the British Legal and Justice System, and how he managed to get a loophole changed in the law.

I received a phone call from Humphrey while I was attending the wedding of my cousin, Kevin Monaghan, which was being held in Balbriggan, North County Dublin. I was asked if I would go down to Dublin the next day to meet Enda Kenny and Fergus O'Dowd at Leinster House (which houses the offices of the Irish Parliament).

Naturally, I was only too pleased to accept and meet the politicians and tell them my story. I arrived at Leinster House at 11.00 a.m. accompanied by John and Humphrey. We were met by officials and led

---

[1] Fine Gael is a centre-right Irish political party formed in 1933. Fine Gael means "Tribe of the Irish".

[2] Enda Kenny (24th April, 1951 -); TD for Mayo since 1975; Minister for Tourism and Trade between 1994 and 1997; Leader of Fine Gael since 2002; Taoiseach since 2011.

[3] Fergus O'Dowd (1st September 1948 -); Drogheda Mayor (1977 – 78, 1981 – 82, 1994 – 1995); served on Louth County Council (1979 – 2003); elected as TD representing Louth in 2002; party spokesman on Environment, Heritage and Local Government (2004 – 2007); Transport and Marine (2007 – 2010); Education and Skills (2010-).

to the offices of the Opposition Leader. There we were joined by Fergus O'Dowd, TD[4]. After a very warm welcome and the usual meetings and greetings, we sat down around a table and in a very business-like way, I began to tell them my story in the best way that I could.

They listened intensely to what I had to say and at various points, stopped and asked me questions. I could tell they were both very impressed with what I was saying.

The meeting lasted just over two hours and it was at that time that Enda gave an assured commitment that he would start the process and consult with Government ministers, the Irish Police, the Health Board (including the equivalent to the British Medical Association – the Irish Medical Organisation[5]) to find a consensus that all the parties could sign up too and implement a similar framework that would help pave the way for a change to the drink-driving laws in the Irish Republic.

*

There was a General Election in Ireland on 25th February 2011. Fine Gael made huge gains and was by far the largest party in the new Dial. Soon after the election, the 'horse-trading' began with the other parties to form a new Government, which resulted in Enda Kenny becoming the new Prime Minister and was to lead a new coalition Government with the Irish Labour Party[6].

Enda definitely didn't waste any time and quite quickly into the new Government he got the ball rolling, setting up the process to initiate a raft of changes to the drink-driving laws in the Irish Republic. I was obviously pleased to see that the new Prime Minister was so swift off the mark. In his first few months in power, he was able to install measures that would dramatically change road safety attitudes and that

---

[4] Teachta Dála is a member of Dáil Éireann, the lower house of the Oireachtas (the Irish Parliament). The British equivalent is Member of Parliament.
[5] Formed in 1984 through merging of Irish Medical Association and Irish Medical Union. It is a professional association for doctors in Ireland but acts also as a Trade Union representing doctors in negotiations with the Irish Government.
[6] Founded in 1912 as the political wing of the Irish Trade Union Congress.

potentially would save many wasted lives (which occur all too often on Irish roads and especially car crashes related to drink-driving).

Of course I knew that this would be no easy feat for the new coalition Government, but whilst it is being led by the Prime Minister and the new Minister for Transport, Leo Varadkar[7], it had a great chance of success.

*

Luton, where I live now, has a huge Irish contingent made up of first, second and third generation families who all help to make it the vibrant multicultural town that it is today. The Luton Irish Forum[8] is a locally run community group and charity that looks after the welfare and well-being of the Irish and other ethnic minority groups in and around the town. They carry out a very reliable job for a lot of the vulnerable people who live on their own.

One of the most recent success stories was to repatriate some of the most vulnerable Irish men who were left in this country after their working days were over. These were hard-working men who came over to England at the age of 14 or 15 to look for jobs in, what seemed at the time, a far-off foreign country. They would work mainly in the building trade as bricklayers, plasterers or even labourers.

Vauxhall Motors[9] was a destination for many of the engineering minded men. And many of these men are now in their seventies or eighties. Most got married, settled down and have got strong family support networks. Some of them stayed single and though had a reasonable enough life, somehow ended up living on their own – but whilst they perhaps had many friends, they had no real family or company at the end of their days.

---

[7] Leo Varadkar (18th January 1979 -); TD for Dublin West since June 2007; appointed Minister for Transport, Tourism and Sport in March 2011.
[8] More about the Luton Irish Forum can be found at http://www.lutonirishforum.org/
[9] Founded in 1857, Vauxhall Motors was one of the main employers in the Luton area for many a long year.

Some of these lonely men had never been back to Ireland since the day they left, so this is where the Luton Irish Forum became involved and set up a scheme (with the help of the Irish Government) to start the process in repatriating the men back to where they came from – some from the cities and towns and some even from the villages, in rural Ireland. This has been a great success and I'm sure that a lot of these men wish they'd made the journey home sooner than they did.

Frank Horan, Chair of the Luton Irish Forum and one of the main founders of the LIF (which was set up some 13 years ago), did so with the help of Margaret Moran, MP[10] and Lord Bill McKenzie[11]. They have a very strong hard-working committee, ably led by Noelette Hanley, Manager of the Luton Irish Forum, who does a great job in holding everything together and providing a great service to the community.

What was needed next for the LIF was a new building. Although the existing one faired them well, it was far too small and thus plans were made for a new state-of-the-art home to provide for the great service they delivered.

My friends, Johnny Boyle and his son Stephen, who were strong supporters of the work done by the LIF, got the ball rolling with architects' drawings and subsequent planning permission, and then agreed to carry out the work for cost price. They also received a grant from the Irish Government towards the costs.

Johnny did an amazing job and created a fine building which was three times the size of the old one. It was well thought out, eco-friendly and had a warm and welcoming feeling as soon as you walked through the door. Works were completed in October 2011, but the official opening wasn't to be until January 2012.

---

[10] Margaret Moran (24th April 1955 -); former Labour Party politician; MP for Luton South 1997 – 2010.
[11] Baron McKenzie of Luton (born William David McKenzie; 24th July 1946 -); Labour politician and, until 2010 General Election, had been Parliamentary Under-Secretary of State at the Department for Work and Pensions and Department For Communities and Local Government.

Frank Horan, Johnny Boyle and Enda Kenny are all natives of County Mayo, on the west coast of Ireland. A plan was put together to invite Prime Minister Kenny over to Luton for the official opening of the new building – and this is where I became personally involved.

I was asked whether I would be the one to ask Mr Kenny to attend, as I had met him previously. We put together a letter of invitation and this was sent to him via Bobby McDonagh, the Irish Ambassador to the United Kingdom.

Within a fortnight, and to our great surprise, he accepted saying he would be only too pleased as it was an honour to be invited. He added that he would confirm his availability in due course.

The date that came back to us through the Irish Embassy was 12th January 2012 and this would also be the first state visit of an Irish Prime Minister to Luton. What a coup that was to be for the Irish community living in and around the area.

A great day was had by all and although it was January, the sun even came out to greet Mr Kenny. The Mayor of Luton, Councillor Don Worlding[12], was there to welcome the Prime Minister, as was Lord Bill McKenzie, himself a former leader of Luton Borough Council.

Bill was a great champion of multiculturalism in the town and was respected by all political parties and by the ethnic minorities who came and settled in Luton. It was therefore appropriate that he made the welcoming speech and thanked Mr Kenny for accepting the invitation and visiting us.

Following Bill's speech, it was time for Mr Kenny to address the large and excited audience. To everyone's delight, he gave a most inspiring speech which focused mainly on Irish immigration over the years. It was one of the finest speeches that I have ever heard from any Irish minister on a visit to the UK.

---

[12] Cllr Don Worlding, elected to serve as a councillor for the Bramingham ward in 1996; chosen to serve the newly formed Northwell ward in 2003; appointed Mayor of Luton in 2011.

Tens of thousands of Irish men and women had made their way across the Irish Sea to find work, earn some money, hopefully buy a house and settle down. Those that did, did so in many towns and cities across the United Kingdom. In 1950, migrant Brian Behan[13] put it best when he said: "For hundreds of years, prime cattle and working men had been Ireland's chief export."

The journey to England across the sea was a short but often treacherous one. The Irish Sea was black, cold and the waves were often as high as houses. One well-known ship that many travelled on was the infamous Princess Maud. This had been daubed the 'Immigrant Ship' and was also nicknamed 'The Wetship'. They said it wasn't fitted with any stabilisers and so it sailed through the water and not over it!

A poem by Frank Horan written back in the fifties captured the scene on the boat perfectly:

Darkness was falling as we rode the wintry seas, The lights of Ireland fading to become fond memories. The Maud was creaking, tossing, lashed by wind and rain, And the sea-sickness gripped us, as our stomachs ached with pain. The feeling it was awful as you tried to keep your head, As you rolled about that bloody boat, you wished that you were dead. Murphy in his agony belched and cried and roared, 'Get me absolution quick' says he, 'for I'm jumping overboard'

The Princess Maud was the same ship that my own family arrived in England from Holyhead in June 1960. My father William had come over to Luton a few years earlier and found a house for us to move into, a three bedroom semi; not quite the size that we needed for a home for my mum, dad and 12 children!

The atmosphere that day in the main hall was mighty. Everyone was so pleased that Prime Minster Kenny had made the journey to Luton and by doing so, it gave such recognition to the work and effort carried out by the LIF.

---

[13] Brian Behan (10th November 1926 – 2nd November 2002); Irish writer; trade unionist; brother to Brendan Behan.

Mr Kenny finished his speech by congratulating the Irish for their contribution to the way of life in the United Kingdom, their rebuilding and reshaping of the new towns and cities, the roads and the railways. The Irish had really played such a major part in many of the infrastructure projects around the country. Integration came easy to the immigrating Irish and this had been proved over so many decades where the Irish and the English have now become firm friends and get on so well that it is very difficult to tell them apart[14].

The downturn in the economy, the banking crisis and the recent financial meltdown has affected both countries very badly and Ireland even more so. The inevitable result of this will be another wave of Irish immigrants crossing the sea to the UK in search of work, but this time they will be highly educated and well trained young men and women hoping for a better future. Once again, history will show that Ireland's biggest export is its youth. But what a shame that these young people can't stay at home to work and build what hopefully one day will be part of their own country's success.

Throughout the day, plenty of beer and wine flowed – but also plenty of water and juices for those who didn't or no longer indulged in partaking of the hard stuff!

The Prime Minister made a point of meeting as many people as he could. It was obvious that he really enjoyed the experience as he was smiling throughout the whole event.

I was lucky enough to have a private audience with him and we discussed how the passage of the new drink-driving process was going on in Ireland. He say that good progress was being made, but there was still a lot of work to do. Details and clarifications still needed to be resolved, but he was confident that there would be new laws brought before the Irish Parliament during the latter stages of 2012.

---

[14] Which was somewhat ironic because it certainly hadn't been easy during those early days when I first came to England. I remember as a boy looking up at a sign on a local pub, The Bedford, which read "No Blacks, No Irish, No Dogs". Racism certainly was rife during the 1960s and 70s.

I offered my services to go to Ireland and meet with any of the groups or organisations that were either supporting or objecting to the new laws that would eventually make the roads in Ireland a safer place to drive on.

He welcomed my offer and encouraged me to visit in the near future so that I could tell my story on how I achieved the changes in the law in the United Kingdom. There were still some people in Ireland who needed convincing that this was the right path to take and why it was so necessary in reducing road deaths relating to drink-driving. We shook hands and agreed to keep in touch, and then we said our goodbyes.

*

It wasn't just the Prime Minister's speech that he made that day that went down so well with all the Irish in the UK. It was also the speech that he had given in the Dial in Dublin a few months earlier that really caught everyone by surprise[15].

He had stood up, and with a prepared speech, he condemned the people who carried out child abuse in schools and government-run institutions during the past century. He condemned the Catholic priests, nuns and teachers who systematically sexually abused and assaulted children in their care. He also condemned the cover up by the authorities and the police, not just for turning a blind eye or even looking the other way, but for being complicit in one of the most appalling episodes of history ever to come out of Ireland.

Mr Kenny missed none in his condemnation, including parish priests, bishops, cardinals, right up to the Pope himself. As far as he was concerned, they were all to blame and carried some responsibility in one way or another. It was now time for them to come out from their hiding places and face justice for the most evil of crimes.

---

[15] The releasing of the "Cloyne Report" (July 13th 2011) highlighted that clergy leaders in the diocese of Cloyne did not act on complaints against 19 priests from 1996 to 2009. The report concluded that the Vatican had encouraged bishops to ignore child protection guidelines.

I hope that the culprits who committed these crimes, and those who covered them up, realise that sins against children and the vulnerable are unforgiveable, and if they cannot be brought to justice on this earth, then they will dealt with on their day of reckoning and God willing, will be sent to straight down to hell.

To the Irish Diaspora around the globe, Mr Kenny's words, although very uncomfortable to hear, I'm sure there was a collected sigh of relief and a weight off the shoulders of all the good people who were wanting this part of history to be exposed to the rest of the world. Finally someone in authority and high office had the courage to stand up and be counted and speak up for all the victims of child abuse, over so many years in the Irish Republic. His estimation as a politician, and as a man, in speaking the truth was raised by a country mile in nearly every Irish person around the world.

The dark clouds of history that had been hanging over the Catholic Church of Ireland for many years are now clearing from the skies and are heading full steam towards the Vatican. It is now up to them to do the right thing and clear up the unholy mess that they have created and tried to cover up. Let us hope that the sex abuse victims and their families can now get on with the rest of their lives – all thanks to Enda Kenny.

After a very successful day, we retired to my brother's pub in Luton, the Sugar Loaf. I arrived there with my friends, Kevin Whately[16] and John Hughes, where we met up with Humphrey Deegan and his friend John Kingston, who was a businessman and friend of the Prime Minister.

We had a few drinks and worked out when a good time would be for my visit back to Ireland to eventually meet with all the groups and individuals who would like to discuss the role that I played in changing the drink-driving law in the UK.

What was to come next was a nice surprise in that myself and Kevin Whately were invited over to Ireland to play golf at the world

---

[16] Kevin Whately (6th February 1951-); English actor.

famous Old Head of Kinsale Golf Club[17] in County Cork. We gladly accepted their kind invitation.

My son Kevin would have loved to have joined us.

---

[17] More about this excellent golf club can be found at: http://www.kinsalegolf.ie/

Chapter One

Grief.

The process of reacting to personal loss.

Yet, grief can be far from normal or predictable, as I sadly discovered to my own cost following the sudden loss of my teenage son Kevin, on Saturday 31st October 1998.

I have experienced all the common emotions of grief including anger, guilt, anxiety, despair and sadness.

I have also endured many of the not unusual physical reactions like insomnia, loss and changes in appetite, dryness of the mouth, shortness of breath and repetitive motions.

However, I also feel that by telling my account of all that has happened since that fateful night, I am also engaging in some very valuable grief counselling therapy and that will certainly help me positively in dealing with my profound personal loss.

*

I was no different to any other parent after the sudden death of their child and found the intense grief unbearably devastating. I have realised also that one way of dealing with this grief is an honest admission that it will probably be a lifelong process.

Throughout my darkest hours, I have fortunately been able to call upon the comforting support of my family and friends, all of whom played a massive part in helping me survive the most traumatic period of my life.

As a major part of my own grieving process, I decided that it would also be a step in the right direction if I returned to Portugal – this was where I'd first heard the news of Kevin's tragic death, following a road crash near Dunstable, in Bedfordshire.

Situated along Portugal's sun-drenched southern coast, the Algarve is every golf lover's idea of paradise. I didn't really need any other reason to choose that particular popular holiday destination in 1998 for my wife Derry, youngest daughter Roisin and then toddler Patrick, to enjoy a relaxing week of playing golf in the glorious sunshine in the company of my wonderful family.

It would take me almost another eight years to return to that part of the Iberian Peninsula, eight years that had been a real positive and life changing experience in every possible sense – strange as that might seem, considering those tragic, tragic events.

Until June 2006, the very mention of the word Portugal would give me an instant 'flashback' of that nightmare experience from eight years previously. So for that reason alone, I felt it necessary for me to travel back to the Algarve to rid myself of those awful demons. Once or twice I had contemplated a return journey but it took all those years to summon up the courage and organise a return trip to Vilamoura, which I eventually did that June.

I had no idea how I would react to retracing my steps in Faro Airport. This was where I had spent a number of frustrating hours on Sunday 1st November 1998. After receiving the news of Kevin's death, I tried to get out of the country as soon as I could - no mean feat as it transpired.

I bit the bullet and booked the flights for Larry Cooney (a journalist from the Irish Post), a good golfing friend of mine, Tony Rudkin, and myself. We spent five memorable days at the Atlantis Hotel in Vilamoura. It was Larry who persuaded and encouraged me while we were away to write down my thoughts and get the book underway.

It was certainly a decision I didn't take lightly, because honestly I didn't know how I would feel on returning to the airport for starters. However, following a conversation with Tony, who had sadly recently lost his wife Ann after a long battle with cancer, we both agreed it would be excellent therapy for the both of us. I did feel it necessary to make that return journey but also that it would do him some good too.

Everything went well during the trip and even though I still recognised certain parts of Faro Airport, I managed to keep my composure despite the odd sudden jump in my heartbeat and shortness of breath.

That was proof, if ever I needed it, that I was still suffering from the pangs of complicated grief. Although I tried my best to hide my feelings from my two companions, my memory of that Sunday morning in November 1998 began to hurt like hell deep inside.

*

Our visit also coincided with the start of the football World Cup in Germany. Happily everything worked out well from the moment we checked into the hotel in Vilamoura, from the courteous hotel staff to the wonderful Portuguese themselves.

It didn't take long before I realised how wrong I had been about my previous perception of Portugal and its inhabitants. What happened to me previously in 1998 wasn't anything to do with Portugal whatsoever and although I didn't blame the country, the sad fact was that anytime that word was mentioned, it immediately triggered nothing but bad memories.

Returning to the Algarve was definitely a step in the right direction and I could have easily have fallen in love with it all over again, especially now when I have successfully buried my demons from November 1998.

We met some great people during our stay, including a lovely couple from Swindon that Tony and I bumped into when we were golfing one time at Villa Sol. That was the round of golf that I was denied eight years previously but after spending a most enjoyable day on the course, it was certainly well worth the wait.

At O'Neill's (one of the two recognised Irish pubs in Vilamoura) one evening, we met players from the County Mayo Gaelic Football Team along with their manager, Mickey Moran. According to Mickey, a Derry native, his charges were not on holiday but were on a training break before their next round of the Connacht championship.

Having fulfilled my wish to play a round of golf in the Algarve, my next objective was to return to Carvoeiro, a tranquil and idyllic beach further west of Vilamoura.

Tucked away beneath a cave, my previous visit to Carvoeiro was about the only memory I had cherished from my last visit to Portugal where Derry, Roisin, Patrick and I spent a memorable first day of our holiday in October 1998.

My return in 2006 brought back all those lovely memories of that same day, where Roisin had been running around the same beach all those years previously. I was so glad that I had returned on what was a scorching hot Sunday morning and I left with a firm intention of coming back again with my family sometime in the future.

*

Reflecting as I write this, I can scarcely believe how I managed to successfully cope with Kevin's loss.

Little did I realise what an emotional roller-coaster ride those years would be from the painful experience of suddenly losing a loved one to the immense satisfaction of taking on the complex British legal system and successfully closing a gaping legal loophole in the drink-drive laws.

The emergence of Duggan's Law in 2002 after such a relatively short time frame was an unexpected legacy of Kevin's tragic death, as my primary objective had been to find a fitting memorial for my late son, which I'm sure he would have approved of.

The completion of The Kevin Duggan Golf Academy in Stockwood Park[18], Luton in 2004 was intended to give aspiring young golfers, even younger than Kevin was, the best possible introduction to the sport and who knows, even one day produce Britain's answer to Tiger Woods

While there are many of who will think what my supporters and I have achieved has been quite extraordinary, my personal experiences

---

[18] More about the Golf Centre can be found at: http://www.activeluton.co.uk/stockwood-park-golf-centre/ You can also find the Professional Golfers' Association at http://www.pga.info/ and the Ryder Cup Trust at http://www.rctrust.info/

along with the numerous other problems I have encountered along the way could have happened to anyone.

I certainly don't claim to be superhuman, but if there is one lesson I have learnt, then that is to never accept second best in this life, even if it is from the police service or anyone else in authority.

Britain's overworked police service certainly deserves our full support in maintaining law and order just as much as we deserve the best possible service from them. It certainly gave me no satisfaction to discover that some members of my local police force faltered during the early investigations into the tragedy.

Sadly, even to this very day, it would appear that I still continue to pay for exposing some of the alarming deficiencies and incompetence within my local force. All I ever sought was a thorough investigation of the true circumstances that led to my son's death and I was not prepared to settle for anything less.

As in the case of any tragedy, the best possible legacy or outcome must surely be to ensure that it isn't repeated. If that is unattainable, then the next best objective must be to ensure that such road traffic tragedies occur with less frequency.

The introduction of Duggan's Law, which permitted the blood sampling of unconscious drink-drive suspects as admissible evidence, certainly led to more drink-drive convictions and therefore provides a necessary deterrent for all drivers who attempt to exceed the legal alcohol limit. But, only the presence of more responsible drivers will help to reduce the actual number of road crash casualties.

However, no matter how great your own loss might be, there's always somebody out there who is going to feel they're far worse off than you.

On attending a Road Safety Campaign[19] event in Bedford in 2003, I met an unfortunate man who had his entire family wiped out due to the actions of a reckless drunk driver.

---

[19] For about road safety campaign organisations, please see Appendix.

That particular man, who lost his wife and two children (a son and a daughter), came along to the Road Safety Campaign meeting purely to enlighten all of us present about a serious case of police incompetence, whilst investigating his own case.

Because the investigating officers lost the paperwork and evidence against the charged driver, the prosecution had to settle for an acquittal. This meant the driver was allowed to leave the court free to ride off into the sunset. I was greatly inspired by this brave man's battle and felt fortunate that I was not going to allow the police force to treat me in the same way.

Looking back now, it has therefore not only been quite a journey but also a long healing and therapeutic process. In many ways, my Road Safety Campaign work, along with the extensive fundraising programme, has been the perfect antidote to take my mind off the full extent of my grief.

When I see parents who suffer a similar sudden loss of a child, I feel I am certainly well qualified to empathise with them. TV viewers could not help but be moved by the reaction of Bill Hawker in March 2007 to the news of his murdered daughter and teacher, Lindsay, in Tokyo. His only comfort was to vow a carry a photograph of her forever and not rest until his daughter's killer was caught.

That was exactly how I felt when I discovered that the driver of the vehicle in which my son died was not prepared to accept any responsibility for his dangerous and even reckless driving on that horrific night in October 1998.

Securing a successful conviction was not going to bring Kevin back, but I felt I owed it to him, not to mention the safety of all road users to ensure that justice was done.

I believe that by telling others of my experiences, I will provide an appropriate final chapter of this sad, but all too common story.

As a successful publican in Dunstable for over 20 years, I know full well how alcohol can dominate certain individual's lives. Sadly, drinking to excess is still regarded as 'cool' for far too many young people, but one only has to look at the consequences of alcohol abuse to see how many of these lives can be ruined forever.

I am still coming to terms with the fact that I have been such a central figure in what I believe has been a powerful story.

Hopefully, it will go some way towards improving the awareness of the effects of alcohol abuse.

I sincerely pray that the achievements of my friends and I will be a real source of inspiration for anyone who ever finds themselves in similar adversity.

Chapter Two

My son Kevin was only 19 when he was killed instantly in a road crash on Saturday October 31st 1998. The second eldest of my three children with now ex-wife Linda, his untimely death has left a permanent void in my life, despite the fact that I also have five other beautiful children. Kerrie and Roisin are sisters of Kevin, while Patrick, Danny and Sinead were born to me by second wife, Derry.

Kevin and I had an exceptionally close father–son relationship. In fact, we were like friends or even brothers. As he got older, I always treated him like an adult. Our relationship also deepened as a result of the early stages of my divorce from his mother.

Having to go through a separation and difficult divorce had also quite a devastating effect on my life. Had it been my choice, the divorce would probably never have happened but on reflection it was the right decision for both Linda and I.

At that time I did all in my power to salvage the marriage but sadly it was all to no avail. Missing the daily contact with my children, Kerrie, Kevin and Roisin, was undoubtedly the most painful aspect in those initial stages of the separation. The daily routine of having to wake them up in the morning, getting them ready for school and then coming home in the evening to sit around the dinner table – all those things which seemed so natural for a normal family unit were now missing.

The immediate effect of the separation meant that I had to live alone in the living quarters over my pub, The White Swan in Dunstable, Bedfordshire. The loneliest thing every night after last orders, clearing the pub and locking up for the night was not having the company of my children to give goodnight kisses too.

Ask anybody who has been through it and they will tell you that divorce is certainly one of the most traumatic experiences one ever goes through in their life.

Saying that, although it was a very dark period, quite ironically, it also saw the beginning for me of an even deeper relationship with my children.

As I said previously, I really missed the regular daily contact despite the fact that they lived in the family home, which was only 200 yards from the White Swan.

Kevin was about 10 or 11 at the time of the separation, so I decided I would make a special effort to do things that I could share with my family. Some activities or sport that I would have in common with him appeared to be the most obvious solution.

Golf was the answer. Kevin was keen to learn and I had high hopes that Kerrie might also be interested. But at 12, Kerrie understandably had other social interests.

And how those interests have blossomed! After leaving Manshead Upper School in Dunstable at 16, she then attended Luton Sixth Form College and completed a two year course in Performing Arts, Dance and Drama.

After various jobs and positions, Kerrie got a lucky break and was invited over to Dublin to audition for a role in a Jim Sheridan[20] film called *The Boxer*. She got the part and loved the whole experience of being on a movie set. A year later, she was invited back to work for Ardmore Studios but this time on the other side of the camera.

From there Kerrie went on to university, got her degree and decided to travel the world for a while. On her return, she soon set up her own dance and drama school, where she produced, directed and choreographed her own shows in theatres around Luton and Dunstable. Her next project is the writing of a musical play, which will be staged at the newly built Grove Theatre in Dunstable.

Kerrie got her introduction into dance when joining the Sheila Coxhill School of Dance at the age of three. Roisin soon followed her

---

[20] Jim Sheridan (6th February 1949 -); Irish film director; six-time Academy Award nominee; perhaps best known for his films *My Left Foot, The Field* and *In America*.

and went on to become a fine dancer with great potential and now my youngest daughter, Sinead, has followed them both into the world of dance and also joined Sheila Coxhill in 2011.

But I digress. Kevin and I began by frequenting a great little golf course at Redbourn Golf and Country Club[21], which was quite convenient to Dunstable.

At Redbourn, we met an impressive young female professional named Gerry Teschner, who hailed from Redcar in the North East of England. Gerry was a regular in the White Swan and a number of times we had spoken about the possibility of taking golf seriously. Kevin and I subsequently became regulars at Redbourn where we had lessons together. Gerry proved to be an expert tutor and put us through programmes and exercises so we both began at the same standard and finished up at the same level of ability.

Our golfing experiences were the perfect platform in which we got closer to one another as we enjoyed some tremendous banter and side bets on our prowess and progress in the sport which we had both grown to love. No serious money ever changed hands but we did bet on certain things and Kevin would beat me as often as I would beat him. A great competitive streak developed between us.

Golf was becoming an important part of our lives especially the sheer fun element of it and when it came to participating in tournaments and great weeks away from Dunstable.

Since Kevin and I were also becoming quite good at it, we received invites to tournaments with various societies including the brewery which was attached to the White Swan.

Kevin really loved these events and I remember on one particular occasion, when he was about 13, going to a town in nearby Shefford to Beadlow Manor Golf Club and Health Fitness Centre[22] one weekend. It was there he enjoyed his first massage and like all of us, he loved being pampered.

---

[21] More about this golf club in St. Albans can be found at http://www.redbourngolfclub.com/

[22] More about the hotel and golf club can be found at http://www.beadlowmanor.co.uk/

A trip to the USA to watch the Republic of Ireland play in the 1994 World Cup Finals is also another cherished memory. That was at a time when I was courting my future second wife, Derry, who joined Kerrie, Kevin and I on the trip. Young Roisin remained behind in Dunstable with her mother.

Kevin and his cousin John Higgins, my friend Jim Morris and I were first to fly to New York where we stayed at the Journey's End Hotel in Midtown Manhattan. We stayed for a week and had a great time. We also visited a number of our relatives, in particular Martin Kelly. We took a private plane to Boston and then onto Martha's Vineyard where we had an amazing time dining in some of the nicest restaurants on the planet as well as taking in all the history and heritage. It was easy to see why it was such a favourite holiday destination for the likes of the Kennedys, the Kellys, the Clintons, Frank Sinatra and all the wealthy Irish families from the East Coast of America.

Martin Kelly was one of the most interesting men I have ever met. We called him Uncle Martin but he was actually a cousin. His mother Rose and my grandmother Mary, along with one other sister Maureen, had the surname of Long. The Longs came from Barnaderg in the same part of Galway as the Duggan family.

He was really like an uncle to us all. Uncannily he looked just like my dad, with the same features and manners. They also had the same sense of humour. In fact, thinking about it, he looked more like my dad than his own brothers did! It was a terrible shame that we did not get to meet him and his family sooner in our lives than when we eventually did.

It was around 1990 when I first met Martin, in Boston, Massachusetts. I was 34 at the time and he would have been about 78. My father, Bill Duggan, had passed away about a year earlier at the age of 77. Bill was a real hero in our household, hard-working, a very fair man with a strong feel for justice. It was sad that Martin and my father never did actually meet.

Martin Kelly was a very wealthy man who came from humble beginnings in the south side of Boston. Boston was a rough place at that time and therefore he had a tough upbringing. He ended up on the wrong side of the tracks and spent a few years behind bars (or in the can, as they say in the States!).

He started out his working life in the building trade, as a plasterer (like his father). After a while he found ways of making a living without all the hard graft that went with working on building sites.

It was dark times in America in the twenties, thirties and forties. Prohibition had been imposed on the nation; it was known then as a noble experiment. Martin used his wits and found an easier way to make money in the newly formed bootlegging trade.

Smuggling booze into the USA became big business and the route travelled began in Canada and came into the America via the state of Illinois.

Joe Kennedy (the father of the political dynasty of John, Ted and Bobby) also hailed from the same area of Boston as the Kelly family. They say in those parts that most of the Kennedy's wealth came from smuggling, mainly whiskey, across the border into America.

Martin was a great storyteller and he amused us for hours on end, recollecting on his childhood and youth growing up in those terrible times. One of the best stories that he liked to tell was when he became rivals with the Kennedys in this lucrative new business and in the rush to get whiskey and beer into the alcohol-free population of North East America.

Joe Kennedy was not well liked in the Boston region, even amongst many Irish, because it was said he treated the Irish immigrants like slaves and many of boarding houses were nothing better than slums.

He overcharged for everything and was quick to throw families out on the streets when they couldn't pay their rents. The word at the time was that he was in league with the devil himself!

Even those in authority didn't have time for him and the police force, who weren't on his payroll, would do all that they could to disrupt his illegal activities.

Martin went on to tell us about a great 'sting' that he arranged with the help of the local police. They would supply him and his crew with official police uniforms that could then be used to stop the convoys of illegal alcohol that was being rerouted from Chicago to Boston.

He added that it was one of the best feelings he ever had, that they could take all Kennedy's illegal cargo and sell it on for himself and his crew, knowing that Joe Kennedy couldn't report the crime and the loss of his goods.

Martin duly paid the cops and everyone except the Kennedys were happy. Prohibition came to an end in 1933 when the legalisation of alcohol was passed. A whole new industry was created in the brewing and distribution of whiskey and beer. This in itself created tens of thousands of new jobs throughout the United States. This was an important move at this time because the stock market crash of 1929 had caused the Great Depression and another dark chapter of American history.

Some years later, Martin gave up his illegal activities and went into the pub and bar business. He brought his first bar in South Boston in 1949. He owned several drinking establishments, the most popular ones were the Showboat and the Big M in Massachusetts Avenue.

Jazz music was all the rage at that time. Ella Fitzgerald and Louis Armstrong performed regularly at the Big M and they became good friends with Martin. In 1968 he brought the Sportlite bar in 232 Old Colony Avenue, South Boston. He converted, refurbished and extended the bar and it was renamed Kelly's Cork and Bull.

This bar went on to become a legendary landmark and watering hole with generations of the Irish in South Boston. It was a great pub and we spent many a great night there. There was always music, the food was good and the craic was mighty. My brother Vivion liked it so much that when he refurbished his pub, the Black Bull in Luton, he renamed it Duggan's Cork and Bull.

The most prestigious and high profile bar that was in Martin's portfolio was the Durgin Park. It was nestled nicely in the quaint

Quincy Market in downtown Boston, next to the historical civic building Faneuil Hall.

Durgin Park was by far the most popular bar and restaurant. It was situated over five storeys. The Oyster Bar in the basement was a haven for the seafood lovers and it was most famous for its New England crab and Boston chowder.

The few years that we had together were amazing. Martin was generous to all us Duggans. We visited Boston many times and at a drop of a hat he would drop everything and fly us down to Martha's Vineyard to stay at his holiday home at Tashmoo Cove in Vineyard Haven.

We had great days driving round the vineyard and even better nights in the Black Dog Bar and the Blue Canoe Waterfront Grill.

But, the best was yet to come when Martin invited us down to Miami to stay in his Bal Harbour holiday home. It was called Admiralty Apartments, 10160 Collin's Avenue in Dade County, Miami. This was opulence and luxury at its very best.

Martin would often take us to his favourite watering hole Wolfey Cohen's Rascal House where people would queue up for hours for one of their famous salt beef sandwiches, and for an evening out he loved to take us to Joe's Stone Crab on Miami Beach.

I've never seen a restaurant so big, so busy and yet so good. They say the waiters there were earning a $1,000 a night in tips! Martin was well known in these parts and the maître d's in the restaurants always made Martin most welcome. He never had to stand in line and always got the best seats in the house. Similarly, he would think nothing of giving $100 tips to the waiters or waitresses. So as you can imagine he always got looked after the best and treated so well; he was always addressed as Mr Kelly.

One day while sitting around the pool in the Bal Harbour apartments, we were approached by what I can only describe as a beautiful and elegant lady. Although in her 'golden years' she had the look of a film star or princess about her. She overheard us talking about things back in Ireland and England and asked us where we'd come from and whether we were on holiday.

We had a great conversation which lasted a few hours. She was fascinated by the storytelling and about how things were in the United Kingdom, but especially she liked the stories of us growing up in Ireland. She was very kind, she offered us drinks and made us lunch and what followed was many more questions. She didn't give very much away about herself and we felt we were in the presence of royalty. She had an aura about her. She spoke very well and was very easy on the eye.

She would only say that her name was Liz. When she left us and went back to her apartment, Martin told us who she was. Lizanne LeVine and she was married to one of the richest men in America, but that didn't mean anything to us.

She was formerly known as Elizabeth Anne Kelly, sister of Grace Kelly, the famous Hollywood film star of the fifties and sixties who went on to become Princess Grace of Monaco following her marriage to Prince Rainier.

It was then the penny dropped. She was as beautiful as her sister. She had such a nice way about her; elegant, sincere, extremely attractive and, most surprisingly, a very good listener. She joined our company for the few days that we were around the poolside at Bal Harbour.

Martin knew my son Kevin and had met him several times, both in the US and on his visits to England and Ireland in 1996.

While in England, he stayed with me in the apartment above the White Swan Inn in Dunstable. Martin needed a good guide to show him around the town and so Kevin was appointed to carry out that duty. Kevin took him around and showed him all the sights as Dunstable has a lot of medieval and Roman history. Martin, like a lot of Americans, lapped up the history and stories from the area.

Kevin was always willing to oblige. As I found out later, Martin was giving him tips of $50 everytime he showed him around. Kevin knew a good thing when he saw it and I was pleased they got on so well. Kevin was also lucky enough to visit all the places that we had been invited to in the States: Boston, New York, New Hampshire, Martha's Vineyard and Miami.

Martin always made a fuss of Kevin when they met up. When Martin finally got to hear the sad news about Kevin and how he was killed, he was devastated. He called me on the phone from Boston; I could tell in his voice that was one call he didn't want to make. There was a tremble in his voice but what could he say? Only that he was a great kid and he liked him dearly and he was devastated to hear the news. He finished up by offering to help in any way he could but we knew how difficult that would be by being so far apart.

Kevin had a good way about him and that had an effect on many of our relatives. He was so easy to get on with and had a good sense of humour.

It was to be a few years until I next met Martin in the States, again in Bal Harbour in Miami. We had a good talk about Kevin. He was very reassuring, very sympathetic and said with all sincerity that all you could do was take each day at a time and see where that takes you.

As I said previously, Martin was a dead ringer for my dad and they could both turn things around, no matter how bad they were. I think what was comforting for me, and as strange as it seems, was that it was like having my dad around all over again. It was all quite surreal.

I was so glad to have met Martin and to have spent a few years getting to know him. Not only did Martin and my dad look and act like twins, they were almost identical in age. Martin was born in Boston on 5th May 1912 and my dad was born in Galway 9th May 1912 and so this May 2012, they would have celebrated their 100th birthdays.

The similarities too between our two families were uncanny. The Kellys were a family of builders and so were the Duggans. We went on to become prominent publicans with bars, restaurants and nightclubs, as did the Kellys. We lived on different sides of the Atlantic Ocean and had never met each other until Martin visited Ireland back in 1989 and that happened to be the same year that I opened the White Swan Inn in Dunstable. It was quite unbelievable that the two families could take the same journeys in life while living so far apart and not knowing one another at all.

Martin was so kind and generous to us Duggans; he really did feel passionate about finally finding a long lost family. He went on to give us the keys to his holiday apartment in Miami to use whenever we wished. We did take him up on that offer and used the apartment in Bal Harbour many times. Sadly, Martin passed away in 2005 aged 93, but we have still kept in touch with the Kelly clan.

*

Unsurprisingly, the real highlight of our trip to the Big Apple was our visit to the Giants Stadium in New Jersey to see Ireland's memorable 1 – 0 victory over Italy. It had already felt like the Republic of Ireland had won the World Cup, especially after the party we enjoyed in downtown Manhattan later that evening.

This was easily one of the greatest couple of weeks Kevin and I had ever spent together and I still treasure the photographs we took on that memorable holiday. One of the Italian restaurants we dined in during our stay in New York was Dominick's in Little Italy. It was one of these old styled restaurants with just rows and rows of long tables covered with red and white chequered tablecloths. It was also infamous for being frequented by one of the notorious New York crime gangs of Italian ancestry. Despite the football result, we were made to feel extremely welcome and could not have wished for better hospitality during our visit. Singer and actor Dean Martin was also a regular.

These were just great times and we also took up skiing. Although playing golf week in, week out brought Kevin and I together more and more and allowed us to enjoy the best possible quality time together. Another friend and fellow publican, Dave Flynn, introduced us to skiing. Dave, who was also going through a divorce at that time, often called to see me at the White Swan and invited me to join him with a group of his skiing friends.

I can vividly recall our first skiing holiday in Austria, accompanied by Kevin and Kerrie. During the first year of the separation from Linda, a trip like this was a rare and ideal opportunity for us to do things together and consolidate my relationship with them. Being a publican, there was always the temptation for me to have easily sunk into depression and taken a downward spiral with excessive drinking but I decided to be strong for my children, if nothing else.

Kevin became a fantastic skier and it seemed to come quite naturally to him. We started off having lessons together that first time in Austria and then went to Romania, Bulgaria, Andorra and, the best of all resorts, the Sierra Nevada Mountains in Spain, and went there three times.

Roisin started off quite early too, at the age of four in fact, when we went on our second skiing holiday to Romania. Kerrie also became a very good skier as well and just like all kids, they seemed to pick it up a great deal quicker than us adults. We did have some amazing times with all the different families and groups of people. Thinking about these trips brings back some fantastic memories but sadly I haven't been back to the ski slopes since the tragedy in 1998.

As well as his sporting prowess, Kevin was also a smart lad, a very quiet and unassuming sort of boy. He always seemed relaxed, if not too laid-back on occasion. But he was no different to other teenage boys of that time, though he did take an interest in college and his academic studies.

I will admit, whilst he was quite intelligent, he didn't apply himself as well as he should have. Subjects that he enjoyed, he excelled in, whereas those he didn't have the aptitude for, he wasn't quite as good. Most growing teenagers are like that I guess. but I'll admit it did sometimes frustrate me at the time! At least though I helped in getting him his first job, as an engineering apprentice.

One of the White Swan regulars, Ian Fletcher, owned a local engineering factory and subsequently Kevin got his first start on the employment ladder. Ironically, it was probably one of the worst things I could have done for him because he hated that job so much, right from the first day. Try as he might, he just didn't like the work, the company and the people that worked there. There was nothing I could really do to change Kevin's opinion because he hated it with a passion but he did stick it out for a year before finally deciding enough was enough.

As was so typical, he didn't rest on his laurels. He went off and got himself another job with someone who also happened to be a great friend of mine, Danny McIlroy. Kevin's engineering background stood him in good stead for his next job, at Houghton Regis. Danny highly recommended him to AJC Trailers, which sadly also turned out to be his last.

But at least while he was there, Kevin enjoyed considerable job satisfaction working under the supervision of Kevin Daly, making steel and aluminium plates for the fast food catering industry and was very popular amongst the staff. I will never know I suppose, whether he ever forgave me for getting him that first job and giving him his first taste of the 'real world'.

Kevin was a good conscientious worker and when he applied himself he could turn his hands to literally anything. He was just one of those boys that was very adaptable and amenable, that would do anything quite willingly and was always very obliging.

He would also work occasionally at the White Swan, doing mainly cellar duties, progressing through to serving and some real bar work. Although he really liked it at first, he finally agreed that he would much prefer to be on the other side of the counter.

Nevertheless, Kevin was very popular in the pub and was very good with the customers who loved his joke telling and banter. When not on duty, he would frequently come in and have drinks on the slate, claiming that he had asked my permission when he definitely hadn't. We sometimes had a couple of minor disputes over this practice but it was never anything serious.

However, one of my real regrets which will forever stay with me was that we had one such disagreement during our final meeting before I left for the Algarve. It wasn't until the second or third evening after the tragedy that I actually realised that we hadn't parted on the best of terms.

I hadn't seen Kevin for over two weeks before the tragedy because I had been in Marbella in Spain the week before playing in a golf tournament with some of my pals.

I can recall that last meeting because he knew I was away the following week when my friend Marco Armitrano was relief manager for me. Kevin went to see Marco to ask for a small loan, which he claimed I had authorised. Of course I hadn't but it was something I had been accustomed to accepting as a father.

Although it was no big deal, Kevin was somehow avoiding me during that week in between my trips to Spain and Portugal. He assumed I was going to reprimand him and so he kept away; that was just the way he was. I did make attempts to see him but it was just not meant to be.

I have often wished our parting could have been so much different and what turned out to be our last goodbye could have ended better but I'm happy in the knowledge that there was no serious rift between us at the time of his death.

That was a fact I had to come to terms with when I next saw Kevin in the Chapel of Rest, laid out on a cold slab. Although he looked immaculate and even angelic – that remains my lasting memory of Kevin.

However, I remain eternally grateful for the good times I shared with him in his short life, which are the memories I like to recollect. I often communicate with him privately and he will never be far from my thoughts because I know he is now up there in heaven with my father and mother.

Declan Duggan

Chapter Three

In attempting to retrace Kevin's final hours, I sought the assistance of my daughter Kerrie, Kevin's friend Paul Clayton and Paul Anstey, the surviving back seat passenger from the crash. The day certainly began with him reporting for work at AJC Trailers in Houghton Regis.

Kevin's job sometimes required him to work an occasional Saturday morning. He was a keen, conscientious and diligent worker, held in high regard by his former boss, Danny McIlroy – in fact, it was Danny who had recommended him to AJC Trailers where he worked with Kevin Daly (who is the brother of Mary, my manager at the White Swan for a number of years) and although he'd only been there a couple of months, he was making quite an impact.

Whilst Kevin was working, Paul Anstey confirmed that he and (later driver of the car in which Kevin died) Paul Mason were the first two customers who walked into the Winston Churchill pub in Dunstable at opening time (11.00 a.m.) on that same, wet Saturday morning.

Although Anstey didn't realise it then, their visit to the Churchill was the first phase of what was to be a day-long drinking session.

I cannot be absolutely certain about the exact amount of alcohol that the two boys drunk, but it is nevertheless safe to assume that it would have been well in excess of a dozen pints before disaster struck later that evening.

Despite coming from a wealthy family and never being deprived of any of life's luxuries, Mason is believed to have relied heavily on his friends to regularly loan him money, as well as apparently being a compulsive gambler. So much so, that it was said that he could never pass a fruit machine without putting money in it. Anstey later reported that Mason had such an addiction to these machines that his nickname was 'Bright Lights'.

At the time of his death, it was believed that Mason owed Kevin somewhere between £40 and £70, though Anstey and another of

Mason's friends at the time, Paul Clayton, were convinced that Mason owed Kevin at least £70 due to his alleged gambling addiction!

And, besides his reputation for borrowing money from a number of his friends, Mason never appeared to be too concerned about how long it would take him to repay these loans. Consequently, Mason spent much of his time evading his creditors who were constantly chasing him for their money.

Anstey stated that he and Mason spent all morning at the Churchill, that some other friends joined them, including Scott Morgan, and while they played pool, Mason, as usual, concentrated on the fruit machines.

From the Churchill, they went to Morgan's house to watch TV. However, Mason had also made plans to meet his girlfriend Jo and a friend of her, later that night in the Hungry Horse pub.

Anstey is also believed to have made tentative arrangements to meet a new female acquaintance at the Sugar Loaf pub. That was where Kevin was also dropped off later in the evening, just after 8:30.

It is quite possible that once Kevin met up with the boys, he may have drunk one or two pints of lager. No doubt either he would have asked Mason for all, or at least some, of the money owed to him, but after spending much of the day feeding the fruit machines, not surprisingly, Mason didn't have much cash left on him.

To be expected, Kevin would have been quite annoyed by being left inconvenienced by Mason, which was probably not the first time that this had happened. Mason – now beginning to show the affects of the day-long drinking session – insisted on going to his home in Edlesborough in order, so he claimed, to get some of the money which he said his father owed him. Kevin, concerned that Mason might disappear without paying his debts, decided to go with him.

That day, 31st October 1998, turned out to be one of the wettest days of the year. The persistent and torrential rain all afternoon and evening meant driving conditions were now quite hazardous. However, Mason made no allowances for the deteriorating road conditions.

Although the banter between all three boys had been quite light-hearted earlier in the evening, due to the pressure that Kevin had been forced to apply on Mason to recover some of his money, it was now evident that the 'well-intoxicated' driver was becoming quite agitated.

Mason, with his two passengers aboard his Ford Mondeo, set off to his father's home, opposite The Bell. He parked in the pub's car park while he called at home. Neither Kevin nor Anstey left the vehicle. Not evident at the time, there is now every indication that Mason had no intention whatsoever in obtaining any of the money. According to Anstey, it would seem that Mason's only real reason for going home was to get some keys from his sister.

When Mason finally returned to the vehicle after about ten or so minutes, Kevin heard the bad news that he wasn't going to get any of his money. Neither Anstey nor I can be certain why Mason was unable to pay Kevin, but Kevin was quite annoyed with Mason's attitude, especially when this was the same man who was able to drink and play fruit machines all day but couldn't repay his debts.

*

It was now fast approaching 10.00 p.m. and the boys decided to leave Edlesborough for the three-mile return journey back to Dunstable. Personally, I can't understand why Kevin continued to remain in Mason's company at this stage. Surely he must have realised that Mason's driving was beginning to become more and more erratic, and even quite dangerous?

Allowing for the fact that they would be driving along a mainly rural country road and then a dual carriageway, the poor conditions meant that any rational driver would have had to have been extra vigilant and careful. However, by spending most of the day on the drink with only a limited food intake, Mason's physiological condition would surely have been approaching an advanced state of inebriation.

Also, apparently part of the boy's drinking-up ritual in any pub they visited usually involved a game of 'shot gun' whereby the winner of the run back to the car would sit in the front seat.

Unfortunately for Kevin, winning the race from the Sugar Loaf back to Mason's car resulted in fatal consequences for him. That was why Kevin was travelling in the front seat at the time of the tragedy. Little could Kevin have known that by winning the race, he had also just signed his own death warrant.

As Anstey jumped into the back seat, Kevin sat directly in front of him and, as usual, fastened his seat belt. Kevin always did this, but ironically, on this occasion, it was something that may have cost him his life.

An increasingly incoherent Mason never even bothered to attempt to belt up before switching on the ignition as they set off on the last leg of their fateful journey back to Dunstable. As was discovered later, Mason's own negligence proved to be the hand of fate that probably saved him.

Setting off from Edlesborough in the torrential rain, Mason drove towards the Pine Trees / Traveller's Rest roundabout. There, he turned left onto the Tring Road, a narrow but straight country lane with no lighting of any description[23] and also little traffic. It would not have taken Mason long before he gathered speed in his Ford Mondeo Sport.

This route would have taken him past a number of farmers' houses, including Crosswater Farm, and by now, it is more than likely Mason may have been swerving from one side of the road to the other. According to PC Coneely, who was on call-out duty (for a reported farm machinery theft) and also on observation on the Harling Road at the next junction (known as the Plough roundabout), Mason approached the junction at such a high speed, he almost collided with the kerb.

Unsurprisingly, Anstey has little recollection of their one and a half mile journey to the crash scene, it is pretty much taken as read that both he and Kevin were screaming at Mason to slow down and appealing to his better nature to take it easy. The erratic nature of Mason's driving led to PC Coneely leaving his observation post and giving chase.

---

[23] True to this day!

Later, I was fortunate to receive a reliable account of the worsening standard of Mason's driving from PC Coneely. Although Mason's appalling driving record was well known by the local force, he still drove arrogantly and without due care on the roads, despite having two speeding offences and a previous drink-drive conviction.

From what we now know, it appears that Mason was aware that a police car was chasing him, but that didn't stop him and he continued to race along the road.

After his narrow escape at the roundabout (which is now the location of the Monsoon Indian Restaurant), his luck finally ran out at the entrance to the London Gliding Club on the Tring Road, at Wellhead.

Travelling at up to 80 miles per hour in the appalling wet conditions, Mason's Mondeo continued to swerve from side to side as the road now entered a dual carriageway for about a quarter of a mile ending just before the entrance to the club. As the car descended down a steep dip in the road, at the end of the dual carriageway, Mason hit a kerb adjacent to a horse riding sign and completely lost control.

The vehicle may have somersaulted at least once, spun around twice, ending up on the other side of the road facing the club entrance. There it just missed the gateway before finally colliding with a tree, which is still there today.

Kevin didn't stand a chance as he took the full impact of the tree and died instantly from a broken neck. Because Mason had not been wearing his seat belt, he was forced into the passenger seat, behind Kevin's body.

Mason was left unconscious, as was Anstey (who ironically had only recently recovered from another road traffic crash on the night of his 18th birthday a few weeks previously!).

PC Coneely was the first police officer on the scene. Although, I did not discover this fact for some weeks after the crash, I will always remember what he said to me on making his grim discovery, namely:

"The smell of drink nearly knocked me over!" Proof if ever it was needed of what was the root behind the tragedy.

Although Anstey became trapped behind the passenger seat, those on the scene didn't find Mason for some time afterwards. In fact, it was initially believed that the driver might have escaped on foot which is why the assistance of tracker dogs and the police helicopter was summoned.

Mason was eventually recovered underneath Kevin's lifeless body almost half an hour after the crash. It was therefore ironic that not only did Kevin have to take the impact of the tree but also the full impact of Mason's body, as he had not been strapped into his seat.

Anstey's account of the crash is understandably rather sketchy as he was drifting in and out of consciousness at the time. He does remember the moment when he heard the fire brigade cutting the roof off the car in order to free him and that was actually the last thing he clearly recalled before being taken to Luton & Dunstable Hospital.

Later, he also remembered Mason speeding along the dual carriageway, hitting the central reservation and then seeing the tree at the entrance to the Gliding Club just before the impact. Anstey said that both he and Kevin were shouting at Mason to slow down but their cries fell on deaf ears – clearly Mason's recklessness had fatal consequences.

Anstey still has bad nightmares and flashbacks from the horrifying ordeal. Who can blame him?

After regaining consciousness in hospital, Anstey was told that his two companions were in different sections of the hospital. Because of the nature of his own injuries and fractured bones, he was in the orthopaedic ward. He continually asked about the condition of Mason and Kevin, but the doctors or nurses wouldn't tell him.

The next day, Anstey's first visitors included two police officers, who insisted on asking him question after question. Still not knowing the condition of his two friends, he later admitted he was not in a very co-operative mood. In the absence of any support or even a friendly face, two police officers were the last people he wanted to see at that time.

As was later to be revealed, the real purpose of the police officer's visit was to break the bad news about Kevin's instant death and Mason's serious injuries. Anstey's reaction to the tragic news was to cry uncontrollably.

The real irony of this particular crash was that neither survivor was wearing a seat belt, whereas Kevin was.

From the facts collated from the scene of the crash, his body mass probably saved his two friends from the impact with the tree.

Some consolation.

Chapter Four

I had often longed to go to Portugal but it was only in late October 1998 that it actually became reality. Before I left for the Algarve however, I also spent a week away from Dunstable in Spain, golfing.

I was fortunate during that time to have a reliable relief manager in my brother John, which meant I knew I wouldn't be contacted unless it was in case of an extreme emergency. Another brother, Liam, and his wife Fran had been on holiday from Perth, Western Australia and were also staying at the White Swan at the time.

As I went more or less straight from Spain to Portugal, I didn't have the opportunity to see Kevin for at least two to three weeks before his untimely death.

Derry, Roisin and Patrick had been looking forward to our sunshine break in the beautiful resort of Carvoeiro. We stayed in a lovely apartment with every facility one could wish for in order to have a perfect holiday, including lovely swimming pools and sandy beaches.

I can vividly remember that fateful Saturday. For instance, when we were driving out to a beach, I received a telephone call from Hugh Mulligan, one of my account managers from the brewery. He was calling to invite me out to play a round of golf with him back in England.

Naturally, I declined and told him that I was currently fortunate enough to be speaking from the golfing paradise of Europe. We exchanged the usual type of banter and had a laugh and a joke before promising to meet up sometime later during the following week.

The beach we went too was one of the most beautiful I have ever visited. Amazingly, apart from a few other tourists who sounded like they were speaking German or Swedish, we were the only people on the beach, which was nothing short of paradise.

Situated in a remote location that was not even accessible by road, it was necessary for us to climb through some rocks and also a short cave before reaching the beach.

Young Patrick and Roisin had great fun running up and down on the sand. Derry and I just sat and relaxed as we looked out at the sea and watched the tide coming in and out. It was sheer bliss.

Later, after returning to our hotel that evening and once suitably refreshed, we went down to the restaurant. The memories are vivid: Roisin ordering a hot chocolate and as soon as the waiter put it on the table, she accidently knocked it all over herself and burned her leg.

The restaurant staff were ever so good and obliging. I found the courtesy of the Portuguese people really quite striking. They knew exactly how to react and dealt very professionally with the incident by providing water, cloths and ice.

It was a lovely meal after which we relaxed in the nearby lounge and watched TV. Feeling quite tired after our exploits on the beach earlier in the day, we decided to make an early night of it and retired to bed before 11 o'clock.

I also remember not being very familiar with my new mobile telephone. It was the first time I'd ever owned one and so using it was still quite strange to me. I had even been tempted to switch it off while I was sleeping, but because I was so convinced that it wouldn't ring, I decided to leave it on.

It didn't take me long to fall asleep after my head hit the pillow. In fact, I was out like a light within minutes. It was extremely peaceful where we were staying and since I was quite tired, it was also quite easy to get to sleep. However, little did I realise that a few hours later, my peaceful world was going to be transformed into a sheer living nightmare.

*

I had no idea how long I had been sleeping before I could hear the lone sound of my phone ringing. I shall never forget that piercing tone which roused me from my deep sleep.

Despite being semi-conscious, I automatically knew something was wrong. My worst fears were being realised, the most serious personal crisis of my life was about to unfold.

I answered the phone. My brother Liam was ringing from Dunstable and although I was still quite incoherent, I sensed from the tone of his voice that he had some very serious news to tell me. Liam was the first of Kevin's next of kin to be informed about the tragedy by the local police, just before three in the morning.

Liam felt compelled to break the bad news to me as soon as it was possible. Naturally it is very easily to be wise in retrospect, but he probably should have waited until the morning and leave the responsibility to the police to contact Interpol and have them inform me.

Breaking bad news to a relative is never easy. However, to his credit, Liam did his best to comfort and console me after he came straight out with the awful news that the police had just called in at the White Swan.

Those cold words: Kevin had been involved in a fatal road crash and killed instantly.

For anybody who has never suffered from severe shock, I can confirm it is an extremely surreal feeling. One is almost transformed from reality into an 'out of body' experience. I was standing beside my bed when I received the news and my immediate reaction was to drop down in a motionless state.

Physically my body seemed to become a lifeless lump of very heavy meat. I couldn't feel any more. It was as if my whole existence was being drained from my feet through my legs, through my body, my arms and finally my head.

Try and as you might, you simply cannot prepare yourself to receive such devastating news as hearing that one of your children has just been killed. To make matters worse, I was stranded hundreds of miles away from the scene of the tragedy.

A natural reaction is to ask yourself: "Oh, my God! How am I going to deal with this, not to mention the rest of the family?!" I wasn't any different.

I tried to regain my composure and began to think straight and rationally once again, beginning to prepare for the return journey home. Somehow, I had to make every possible attempt to get there as soon as possible.

I began by waking Derry and tearfully informing her of the tragedy. In a shocked state, she also felt helpless as she did not know how to respond except by trying to comfort me in her own way.

However, as our priority was to get to Faro Airport as soon as possible, there was no time for us to reflect wholly on the scale of the tragedy. Our next task was to wake Roisin and Patrick. We decided not to tell Roisin what had happened until we arrived back in England.

Packing our cases in record time despite the shock, we loaded up the hire car for the trip to the airport. After returning the vehicle without too much difficulty, we proceeded to the airport departures where we tried to check in.

Whilst watching the 2007 reports about the awful abduction of Madeleine McCann, I was reminded of the kind of frustration I faced when I attempted to deal with the Portuguese authorities. The McCann's faced all sorts of problems, primarily due to the language barrier difficulties, and that was exactly our problem when I did my best to explain the full extent of my problem and emergency with both airport authorities and the police force.

Explaining my plight turned out to be much more difficult than I ever imagined. Having to approach complete strangers and try to tell officials, who were not even fluent English-speaking, as best I could that I was in big trouble and needed their help.

It was extremely difficult having to inform several people that same terrible news over and over again. It was so frustrating not being able to make any kind of progress those first three or four hours since arriving at the airport.

How often these officials have listened to similar stories is anyone's guess but I was finding it extremely difficult to communicate the urgency of my request to leave as soon as possible. Sadly, my pleas appeared to be falling on deaf ears. I'm even sure some of those that I spoke too must have thought I was making the whole story up! I suspect they were even convinced I was trying it on in order to get an early flight home and that's certainly what it seemed like after speaking to at least three or four different officials. The local police force weren't much better either, as none of them appeared to speak English.

By the end, I was screaming in frustration and pleading with anybody who would listen: my son had been killed and I desperately needed to get a flight back home to Luton, England.

Eventually, I managed to find somebody who was prepared to help. Slowly, they began to grasp the gravity of my situation, and at last I was beginning to make progress and arrangements were put into place. Also, with the assistance of Ken Edge, back in Dunstable, the man who had actually arranged the holiday, we were finally booked on an Italian airline flight back to Gatwick.

I will never forget those painfully frustrating hours at the beginning of our sad, long, journey home. It must have taken at least five or six hours just wandering around the airport, making phone calls, people responding, me calling different people, trying to get us on a flight out of there.

In my opinion, this was where Interpol should have been involved, for had they been, then I'm sure my exit out of Portugal would have been much easier than it ended up.

I have since advised the police that when people travel abroad they should be made aware of the fact that Interpol should be involved in similar cases of emergency. I'm positive it would have been dealt with in a completely different manner i.e. having to explain to four or five different foreign-speaking officials that the urgency of my problem and why it was necessary for me to have to leave the country immediately.

Chapter Five

The Italian airline flight we boarded turned out to be a chartered plane from Faro to Gatwick. Similar to the hours of frustration before we took off, the duration of the flight seemed to last an absolute lifetime.

The whole scene seemed very weird and surreal, from the attire of the cabin crew to the fact that a number of staff didn't speak English.

However, I liked the hostesses knee-length red boots, even if they did seem totally inappropriate. With seemingly the weight of the world on my mind, it was perhaps a welcome distraction for me at that time.

As soon as it was announced we were preparing to land at Gatwick, I then decided to break the bad news to Roisin that her eldest brother had been killed. If I hadn't, it would only be a matter of time before she would have overheard the news when we met those who were waiting for us in the airport. It breaks my heart even now to think about when I told her. That innocent face just stared back at me and nodded that she understood what had been said. During the whole flight, it had gone round and round my head, how do I tell her? What words can I use? But reflecting now, she knew that something awful had happened – she just sat there quietly, waiting for me to say something to her.

Absolutely devastating for the both of us.

My four brothers, John, Vivion, Gerard and Jarlath, along with my friend Marco Armitrano, travelled from Luton to meet us at the airport. Marco had a trolley waiting for us in the North Terminal, and with my brothers, also attempted to comfort us.

It was a very emotional moment for all of us and nobody envied their job. There is no easy way of breaking the news to someone who has just lost a child and that was definitely reflected by the sad and sympathetic look etched on their faces.

The journey back to Bedfordshire took approximately an hour. My first stop was my home in Luton, where Derry and young Patrick alighted before taking Roisin home to my ex-wife Linda's house in Dunstable. Linda wasn't there, so I presumed she might be at her mother's in Beech Green, Dunstable, being comforted by family. That was therefore going to be the next stop.

I took Roisin up the steps leading to the front door. On opening the door, I was met by Linda's sister, Denise. As I looked through the hallway into the front room, I could see everybody was understandably in an extremely distraught state. The setting looked like a scene from a horror film.

There were so many people in that smoked-filled front room, including aunties, uncles and cousins and a God-awful wailing noise. It is a sound I hope I never have to hear again.

What it made it worse was that this house, the home of my children's beloved Nan (Phyllis) was usually a beautiful, loving household. They used to spend every other weekend with her and had so many friends in the area. There was such happiness and joy, and some of their best times growing up were spent there, so to see it transformed like this was truly heartbreaking.

I was told that Linda was upstairs having been treated by her local GP, and may well have been sedated by the time we arrived. Walking up those stairs is now very hard to describe, like stepping into a different place altogether. Taking a deep breath, I finally entered her room.

Linda's bedroom was poorly illuminated, with the only light coming from a bedside lamp. I could barely see her under the covers. When she saw me, she leapt up and attempted to hold me in a comforting embrace.

We were both crying uncontrollably as we tried to come to terms with our profound loss. Sadly, as we were going through a bitter divorce at the time, in our grief we spoke some harsh words to each other. No doubt, we both regret them now. Not wanting to make this bad situation even worse, I decided to leave Linda to it, knowing that we would speak to each other again over the next couple of days.

As I came down the stairs, another door opened and Kerrie appeared. At the time I didn't know she was in the house and this was the first time I'd either seen or spoken to her since Kevin's death. We didn't need to say anything; she rushed into my arms and we embraced each other whilst bursting into tears. After calming Kerrie, I explained that I had to go to the hospital and left Roisin with her. But I assured them both I would speak to them as soon as I was able.

Outside, as I headed to the car, I began steeling myself in preparation for my visit to the hospital in order to see Kevin and hope against hope that some awful mistake had been made by the authorities. I need hardly elaborate as I was quite relieved to have had a perfectly excusable reason for wanting to leave the eerie and even spooky atmosphere. Although I felt terrible about leaving Roisin there, getting to the hospital was now top priority.

*

I returned to the White Swan and after being joined by Vivion, Jarlath and Gerard, we set off for the Luton & Dunstable Hospital.

As is general police procedure, before we could view the body it was necessary to have an officer present with us. Again, it meant having to wait around for a considerable length of time before PC Tony Whinnett arrived. This was to be the same police officer who would be involved in the eventual crash investigation as well as making the road traffic arrangements for Kevin's funeral later that week.

But the time finally arrived when we were invited to view Kevin's body in the Chapel of Rest. It was quite a harrowing experience for all of us to identify and see for ourselves Kevin's body laid out on the cold slab. He was still fully clothed but had obviously been cleaned up.

As I took a closer look at his face, I did see a little blood stain on one cheek. I leant down to hold his cold lifeless body and said a few prayers before giving him a quick kiss.

Jarlath took a note from his pocket (I don't know if it was a five or ten pounds) and placed it in his hand in order to get himself a drink on the 'other side'. I know it may seem quite a strange gesture but certain Irish people do have their own ways of dealing with bereavement.

As we kissed and said our own private goodbyes, we left the hospital to meet up with our other brothers, friends and relatives.

Heading back to the White Swan seemed to be the obvious choice but by this stage I was beginning to feel completely drained by the whole trauma and simply couldn't face any more sympathisers or the many other people who I knew were waiting to see me.

We decided to find some welcome respite at Con O'Shea's pub in Luton instead.

O'Shea's was just around the corner from where Derry, Patrick and I lived. Many of my friends were there, including Dave Flynn and Jim Morris, as well as my five brothers.

Although I was grateful to get away from the White Swan for an evening, I still couldn't avoiding meeting many people I knew who had heard about the tragedy. This meant I was constantly answering the same questions over and over again, such as how I was feeling and when did I hear the bad news etc. etc. The repetition was as excruciating as it was tedious.

I did my best to be polite, puffed out my chest and attempted to breathe without showing my real emotions. Deep down I knew it would soon be time to detach myself from my true feelings in order to start thinking about the long traumatic week ahead of me.

After returning home to Derry and Patrick that evening and feeling absolutely exhausted, my head finally hit the pillow. Despite my obvious fatigue, I didn't get much sleep as I relived all the trauma of the previous 24 hours over and over again.

On the following day (Monday), my priority was to commence with the unenviable task of making the funeral arrangements. Visits to the local parish priest and funeral directors had to be arranged, as well as seeing the investigating officer and car crash supervisor, PC Whinnett.

At least, I had the comfort of knowing that the White Swan was being managed in my absence by my brother John and close friend, Marco. I could therefore concentrate on making the necessary arrangements and doing what needed to be done.

PC Whinnett confirmed to me later at the hospital, just as he had done previously to my brothers Liam and Vivion (as well as to Linda), that Kevin's death had not been the result of an alcohol-related crash.

Although I had no reason whatsoever to doubt that he wasn't a very sincere man, unfortunately PC Whinnett's revelations also proved to be the beginning of a trail of misinformation regarding the circumstances of the tragedy.

But, at that stage, having accepted PC Whinnett's version of events, I was actually quite relieved and had no reason whatsoever to believe that the true facts weren't being disclosed. I believed the circumstances surrounding Kevin's death and the injuries to his two friends were the result of a tragic, tragic accident.

To this day, I cannot be entirely certain to what PC Whinnett's motives were and why he chose to give this version of events. Perhaps it was to soften the blow or perhaps he believed it would be best if the true account of what happened would be better disclosed after the funeral.

Whatever his reasoning, it proved to be a poor piece of judgement on his part because I retained every word he told me in the hospital that day and didn't hesitate to challenge him when the true version of events began to unfold later in the week.

That Monday was also to be the first time that I was going to see my mother, Lena, since the tragedy. She had just flown in from Dublin.

A number of family and friends met at O'Shea's for the second night running. By now the shock of the whole trauma I was suffering was beginning to be replaced by even stranger stress-related sensations which made it extremely difficult for me to think straight.

The effect of Kevin's loss was finally beginning to take its toll and proved to be a heavy weight to carry, not just for me but for his mother, his two sisters and his many friends. However, Kevin's death was a reality. We had to get on and deal with it in our own individual way, no matter how physically and mentally taxing that may have been.

As I mentioned in the opening lines of the first chapter, nobody can account for how one reacts to grief and I was certainly finding it extremely difficult to reconcile the obvious changes that were taking place in both my physical and mental disposition.

My breathing pattern had changed. I could not even lie down properly. Even my posture and the way I walked were different. I started talking with a permanent tremor.

My symptoms were also similar to those who have suffered a stroke. Step by step everything changed for me. My own road to recovery therefore meant learning to walk, talk and even breathe all over again.

There is no easy way to describe the profound depth of my feelings of loss but these were just some of the examples that I was suffering at that time. I also remembered reading somewhere about someone who described quite similar circumstances. It was as if I was walking around with a hole in my chest and each time the wind blew through that hole, it hurt like hell!

That was basically how I felt for a long, long time. After that first Monday evening, the pain didn't ease and neither did my breathing and walking problems. Sometimes it was like I had been lifted off planet Earth and dropped off somewhere really alien. My whole world and life was changed forever.

Indescribable is the only word I can use because I simply don't know of any other words to explain that terrible feeling. I wished for a hole in the ground to open up and swallow me, but I kept telling myself I had to keep going, I had to remain strong.

And besides arranging to give my dead son the best possible send-off, I had many other responsibilities, including the care of my other children. That was perhaps the single thing that kept me going at the time. I also knew that they were very concerned about how I was coping.

Linda was also finding the strain extremely difficult and having to take tranquilisers to cope. I suppose now, even to this day, she has never recovered fully since Kevin's death.

The onus was therefore on me to take the lead in my darkest hour and somehow detach myself from all my own private ailments and problems.

With the help of so many people, including my friends Marco, Jimmy Morris and Dave Flynn, who did not hesitate to take time off work to come to my aid, I set about preparing for the saddest week of my life.

My brothers, and sister Maureen, were also fully supportive in whatever way they could. There was so much to do but at least I was never found wanting for help and support as we set about facing all our friends and sympathisers, as well as making the funeral arrangements.

Chapter Six

Making the funeral arrangements was always going to be a severe test of character. The effects of the shock and the trauma from the tragedy were certainly taking their toll, but somehow I remained strong for the sake of the family. But whilst these arrangements were my top priority, I still felt obliged to attend a number of other issues including the eventual return to the White Swan, which I made, three days later.

I knew that facing the remainder of my family was always going to be a painful experience, but it was a necessity, especially as I needed to talk properly with my mother, who I'd seen only briefly the day before.

Strange as it may seem, it was one occasion when I was not looking forward to meeting with her. I knew she would be devastated - she had also lost a baby son. She never saw young Patrick, who was only three days old when he died. My father was the only person to have seen him, and because of that, my mother kept remembering the baby she had never seen for the rest of her life.

Presumably because Kevin was my eldest son, my mother appeared to have a special affinity with him. How she was going to react to the sad news was something I feared. I knew it was going to be heartbreaking.

I finally met with her at my house in Luton that Tuesday evening, away from the public glare of the White Swan. It was just as expected, tearful and emotional, but as we fought off those tears and attempted to get matters into some perspective, we spoke about what I had been doing and the arrangements I had made.

My mother also wanted to know the full details of what had happened on that Saturday night, and how much I really knew of the facts. I could also tell that she was concerned for my welfare; the stress caused by my grief was beginning to badly affect me both physically and mentally.

Although I was sitting in the comfort of my own lounge, it just didn't feel like it. In fact, it felt like I was actually sitting in someone else's front room. I was definitely becoming more and more detached from reality. Someone else, somewhere else. She didn't even look the same any more. The trauma was beginning to take its toll, that much was certain; after all, my world had completely changed.

I am convinced that she never got over the shock of losing Kevin until her dying day in December 2005. She couldn't bring herself to face the truth that he was no longer with us, and just like her painful recollection of her son Patrick, I often detected a tear in her eye whenever his name was mentioned.

My mother had not had an easy life. Apart from rearing a family of 12 and losing a baby son, she also had to cope with the loss of my father William, affectionately known as 'Billy the Kid' to his friends, some 17 years previously.

Kevin's untimely death was visibly etched onto her face and was clearly having a considerable adverse effect on her health and well-being just as it was on my own physical and mental state. Then in her eighties, it was such a bad time for her as it was for the rest of us. But somehow, we all had to find the strength from somewhere just to get on with life and deal with it in the best way we could.

*

Father Oliver Whyte, an uncle of mine, had also come over from Galway to help out with the preparation of the service as well as some of the other funeral arrangements.

Earlier that day, I had also gone to view the crash scene in order to get some idea of how my son met his end. It certainly was an eerie experience, especially trying to visualise the true circumstances of exactly what had happened that Saturday evening.

I'll be honest, I was advised not to go by the police, but I insisted on being taken to where the crashed car was being examined and inspected.

And, after visiting the crash scene, I was even more determined to see the remains of Mason's Ford Mondeo.

I don't know why I wanted to see the written off vehicle but after persuading the policeman, I was told it would be necessary for him to accompany me to the car. Appearing to be very sincere, caring and obliging, the officer drove me 12 or so miles to the scrap yard in Leighton Buzzard.

Naturally, I was prepared for the worst and although I thought myself just about shock-proof, my first sight of the mangled car left me with an indelible image almost as profound as my first sighting of Kevin in the morgue.

The luxurious and high powered Mondeo was completely unrecognisable. It was literally in bits with one side completely smashed in beyond repair.

Sadly for Kevin, all the evidence pointed to the fact that it was his side of the vehicle that took the full impact of the tree in the crash. His fastened seat belt meant that he would not even have been able to take evasive action before disaster struck at Wellhead. He was the only one wearing a seat belt while the other two, who weren't, somehow and miraculously escaped death. How the driver and other passenger survived and came through their ordeal, God only knows.

*

Just before visiting the crash scene, I decided to drop into the White Swan. Many of my customers and those who had already heard what had happened had been asking after me and so I felt it was time to face all these sympathisers. After meeting a number of different people on entering the pub, out of the corner of my eye I saw one of Kevin's former employers and my friend Danny McIlroy, the man who had recommended Kevin to AJC Trailers in Houghton Regis.

A tearful Danny approached me, but even before we could utter a single word, we were both overcome with emotion. We both regained our composure quite quickly. I was once again obliged to repeat the whole story of the circumstances of Kevin's death.

There were lots of similar meetings like that for me, but it was just a case of trying to be as strong as I could in the face of adversity.

After leaving Danny I took the opportunity to catch up with my brother Liam and all of my staff individually in an attempt for them to come to terms with their loss; everyone in the White Swan was devastated since news of the tragedy broke.

Liam, John, Marco and I had agreed on certain temporary measures but we agreed to run the pub in as normal way as possible and also not to close it on either of the two days of Kevin's funeral.

John and I agreed that everything seemed to be going okay during my enforced absence and so it was just a matter of him checking a few things from time to time. Management standards had to be maintained in order to ensure the pub ran smoothly.

I was thus reassured that the White Swan was in safe hands throughout the immediate aftermath of the tragedy. It was also comforting to know that I was receiving so much great support from all the customers and the staff.

We also received lots and lots of telephone calls from people attempting to contact me. Quite a number of people also delivered sympathy cards or Mass cards to the pub, or personally visited my house. Because I was so pre-occupied with the funeral preparations, I missed many of these caring and concerned callers.

I also began to receive offers of help, telephone calls and letters from people who had been in a similar position to me. I had a visit on Tuesday from Roger Ball, a representative of the Victim Support Road Traffic Services, based in Bedfordshire. Derry answered the door but she sent him away on my request. Initially I was quite sceptical about letting anybody in – it was my mistaken belief that he was nothing more than a nosy parker!

But to his great credit and unbelievable persistence, Roger returned again and, on his third attempt (on Thursday), we relented and let him in. He said that he was there to offer a unique counselling service, a stick to lean on, with someone who was more than fit to advise as he had had a similar experience.

This was to be the beginning of a fantastic two-year relationship of counselling from Victim Support Road Traffic Service. It was a pilot scheme at the time, the only one in the country. I think I was extremely lucky to receive the benefit of this service because a counsellor called to see me weekly for two years after the tragedy.

Roger was a wonderful man, offering me help and relief. The information, knowledge and personal support that he passed onto me was invaluable. He was certainly a man I will never forget and I was delighted to be able to return the compliment in a small way when we offered Victim Support a donation of £15,000 from one of our future fundraising events.

*

No doubt about it, if there are any real positives to be said for funerals or bereavements of any kind, then it is they are always sure to bring together long-lost friends and relatives. People were flocking to see me whom I hadn't seen in years. News of the tragedy had brought so many people flooding back into Dunstable. The procession of sympathisers flocking to my front door was staggering. People came to pay their respects and offer their condolences from all over the country – I was so not used to all that attention.

So many well-wishers came to either my home in Luton or to the White Swan and insisted in paying some form of homage. Although the whole ordeal was so tiring and draining, both physically and mentally, I just had to accept them coming in, shaking my hand, giving me kisses, hugging me. Lots of tears were shed.

But, I tried my very best at all times to maintain my composure, even though inside I was hurting like hell. Usually I showed no emotion until some sympathiser would start to cry and that might be when I would struggle to avoid joining them.

Anybody who has ever had to deal with a family bereavement will know exactly what I and all our close family members had to endure until after the second day of the funeral on the Friday.

Feeling obliged to explain all the circumstances of the tragedy to many of our sympathisers was so hard for all of us directly involved, not only having to come to terms with our loss but also having to relive and regurgitate the facts over and over again.

That is just exactly how it was, but I knew I had to see it through, and that included another night with my chest pounding violently each time I thought about the tragedy and funeral preparation. My breathing patterns were far from regular and as I exhaled, my chest appeared to rise up to eight inches before I could inhale once again.

I cannot explain why my breathing wasn't in tune or what was going on inside my body. But the bad news was that this was only the beginning of my discomfort and so many countless sleeping nights followed. I also felt extremely sorry for Derry who could only just sit there and hear me breathing abnormally because I couldn't sleep.

The weight of responsibility was quite unbearable, not to mention constantly thinking about all the things I had to do, not to mention the repeating flashbacks and remembering that horrifying image of my dead son lying on a cold slab in the morgue.

But, since Dunstable is a relatively small town in Bedfordshire, and Kevin was a local boy through and through, I somehow had to be strong ahead of what was going to be a huge community event.

Since Kevin went to school as well as living, working, socialising in Dunstable, it was inevitable it was also going to be a very sad occasion for the entire community.

One could sense a real chain of emotion and grief developing up and down the High Street and beyond. Much of the local community prepared for one of the biggest funerals the town had ever seen.

I could sense that same feeling all around the town, from the moment I returned from Portugal on the previous Sunday afternoon. I was mindful of that fact and the responsibility I had as I set about preparing to give my son the best possible send off from this life.

Chapter Seven

How can anybody prepare themselves to bury their own perfectly healthy child?

This was the dilemma I faced. Making Kevin's funeral arrangements was such a huge responsibility. However, it did mean that I was temporarily able to take my mind off some of the other more painful post-tragedy issues, a welcome respite.

Amidst the early stages of my grief and trauma after I returned from Portugal, I somehow managed to find the strength to do just that by contacting Dunstable Town Council to arrange the purchase of a burial plot. I then arranged a visit to the local funeral directors followed by a visit to Father Quinn, our local parish priest of St Mary's Catholic Church in Dunstable.

By keeping busy I was able to remain focused in ensuring that I achieved my objective of making sure that everything was going to be done the way I wanted it. Nothing but the best was going to suffice in allowing me to give Kevin the possible memorable funeral.

Still completely unaware of the true facts surrounding his death, I was more than impressed by the support from the local police force who were quite meticulous and courteous in their approach to me. I had no reason to be anything other than grateful for the support I received. They appeared prepared to assist in any way they could.

Again, I cannot emphasise how much help I received from so many people during my darkest hour. It was totally overwhelming. The community spirit and good nature in people usually comes to the force when something like the unexpected and tragic death of my son occurs.

The great and good in my community always seem to want to stand up and be counted when it comes to offering help and there were quite a number of exceptional people around Dunstable during that awful week of my life. Despite the pain, despite the trauma, I still felt that I was such a lucky person to have a tremendous level of support and this was certainly a genuine source of comfort.

But, with good comes bad, but thank God those few were the exception and that fact could not have been better exemplified than at Kevin's funeral.

I shall also never forget my visit to the funeral directors, S.A. Bates, in Dunstable, accompanied by my brother Vivion. The hardest decision we had to make was what type of wood we were going to choose for Kevin's coffin. It was quite a surreal feeling walking around the modern funeral directors and observing the services on offer.

Not demeaning the 'self-service' ambience of the funeral directors, it felt no different than picking out the right pattern of wallpaper or selecting a wardrobe for one's bedroom in a DIY or furniture store.

Selecting the correct type of wood and design finish was really a strange feeling. Since Vivion was a carpenter, he knew exactly how to check the various types of wood. I was therefore relieved to be able to rely on his advice, which included comments such as, "Yes, this is a good one", "This is a nice one" or "This one will last longer", before we finally settled on our decision.

Truly, the whole experience was so bizarre, but we simply had to get on with it.

After visiting the undertakers, the next part of the arrangements was to ensure that I fulfilled my promise to Kevin's mother Linda, by giving our son the best possible tribute, which I began composing on that Monday evening.

I sat down in the back room of my home and jotted down all the years and all the times we spent together during his short life. This included some of the more notable highlights.

The parish priest had agreed that I, and any other representatives from organisations associated with Kevin, could say a few words about him from the altar during the Requiem Mass that coming Friday morning.

I decided to write an abridged version of Kevin's biography. It was an extremely difficult assignment but somehow I found inspiration to actually put pen to paper and finish it.

Many of the anticipated attendants would not have known Kevin personally, which is why I was very detailed in my preparation of his tribute. I drew a little sketch of Kevin's life as best I could in an order that I could readily recall all the wonderful times we spent together. From his birth in 1979 to when he first started primary school at St Mary's in Dunstable, I began to trace Kevin's development from his infancy into becoming a fine-looking young man.

As I've said previously, Kevin loved going to school. His teachers agreed that he was a lovely kid. Very quiet and unassuming, like all diligent students he got on with things and was also very smart.

From his primary school education, right up to leaving secondary, the youth clubs that he went too and the other places he used to frequent, the places where he worked as well as the numerous friends he had made, the football teams he played for - I made a special effort to ensure everybody was mentioned.

I am delighted to say that judging from the positive reaction from those that heard my speech delivered during the funeral services that Friday morning, the final result must have sounded like a fine example of a very poignant, touching, as well as skilfully crafted oratory.

I had definitely felt it necessary to give all those people who were taking the time and effort to attend the funeral the best possible eulogy to Kevin. Apart from the fact that we have an extended family, I knew his popularity within the community would be well reflected by the size of the congregation.

An exceptionally large gathering was therefore anticipated on both the Thursday evening and Friday morning services. The local police were also expecting a large attendance and so they decided to close the adjacent roads in order to ensure the procession could follow the hearse in an orderly way without disrupting too much local traffic both for the walk from the church as well as to the cemetery on Friday morning.

*

Hundreds attended Kevin's reception in the church that Thursday evening (including many working people who would have been unable to attend the burial service on the Friday), followed by a special Mass at St Mary's where his remains reposed overnight until the Requiem Mass that following morning.

I was accompanied to the service by Derry. We sat behind Linda, her mother, her sister and our two daughters. Although Derry returned home afterwards, I went back to the White Swan in order to join some friends and family for a small reception.

Again, I found it extremely difficult to sleep that night as I privately rehearsed in my mind how I was going to deliver Kevin's tribute the following morning during the Requiem Mass. Later, lost in my own thoughts, I did manage it.

*

Another huge attendance filled St Mary's Church as over 1,100 people paid their final respects to Kevin. Although still suffering badly from the effects of his terrible injuries, back seat passenger Paul Anstey also attended the service in a wheelchair before being taken straight back to Luton & Dunstable Hospital. Apart from his sister, neither of driver Paul Mason's parents is believed to have attended the service.

The moment finally arrived for me to approach the pulpit to pay my own final tribute to Kevin before all his relatives and friends in the congregation. A sudden hush descended all over the church as I fought off my nerves, not to mention my very noticeable grief.

Despite my best laid plans to keep the tribute as short as I possibly could, it lasted much longer than expected and therefore made the sermon and Mass run on for some considerable time. But no one seemed to mind, presumably because the assembly couldn't possibly have been more attentive while I spoke.

The celebrant, Fr. Quinn, and all the other priests were also quite content listening to me and all the other speakers.

From the pulpit, I delivered my speech at different intervals before calling on various people who wished to say whatever they felt obliged to say about Kevin. Then, in conclusion, I offered my thanks to the priests and also the local police, not to mention the countless number of other people who had attended, as well as those who had offered their condolences throughout the week since the tragedy.

I remember my closing line that I just now wished to bury my son in order that we could all try to start to live our lives again.

To my utter astonishment, and I certainly cannot ever recall a similar reaction on such a sombre occasion, a rapturous applause broke out which developed into a full standing ovation as I walked down from the altar. The response was appreciated but it was as unexpected as it was nice to receive, but again, it was the only way we all knew to give Kevin the best possible send off from this life.

A similar tremendous response followed for days afterwards with people calling and either personally delivering or sending letters, notes and cards of sympathy. Kevin's Requiem Mass was certainly one of the most solemn and poignant occasions that I am ever extremely likely to experience and judging by the positive reaction, I believe we managed to carry it through with almost impeccable dignity.

Such was the extent of the support at the service, it felt like it was just another of those things that kept me going. One could actually see the strength of people's real emotion that was displayed for our loss. It was so genuine and palpable, you could almost smell it.

As Kevin's coffin, draped in both Republic of Ireland and Celtic football shirts, was taken from the church and placed in the hearse by his pall-bearer cousins, the procession began, a short distance to the nearby cemetery. The police also co-operated by obliging us in closing the thoroughfare.

Led by a lone piper, a cortege of hundreds walked up the main street. As the rain began to fall, we eventually made our way to the cemetery where Kevin was laid to rest.

A lighter moment during the procession occurred when my brother John noticed one of Kevin's friends dressed in unusually short trousers that also exposed a pair of hole-riddled socks. The side-splitting funny incident may have been a welcome distraction but it was only a temporary respite during Kevin's final journey.

My uncle, Fr. Oliver Whyte, presided at the graveside ceremony before blessing the coffin ahead of it finally being lowered into the ground. It was such a moving and sad ceremony not just for the family but for everyone who was present and who had braved the miserable weather.

Without a doubt, that was certainly the moment when I wished that Philip Mason, the father of the driver, would have been present at the graveside. Perhaps then he would have realised the pain and suffering that our family was feeling. He may have well chosen a quite different stance when the time came for his lucky-to-be-alive son to accept and subsequently face up to taking some responsibility for certainly my innocent's son life.

Accomplished singer, and family friend, Ray Howlett, concluded the graveside ceremony with a moving rendition of the 'Old Rugged Cross'. It was such a fitting and sombre finale, which left many of the remaining attendees in tears, as we all said our own private farewells to Kevin – a teenage boy who was so cruelly denied the opportunity of ever fulfilling his full potential.

Now as surely an appropriate time to continue with the celebration of his short life without any unforeseen distraction.

How wrong that supposition later proved to be.

Chapter Eight

Two traditional Irish wake receptions were organised in Dunstable following Kevin's burial. Although everyone who attended the funeral were invited to join us, many had to return to work so thus declined, but those that did remain either went back to the White Swan or the local Parish Hall, next door to St Mary's Church.

Our family had felt obliged to host two wakes, purely to accommodate the large number of people who couldn't get into the White Swan. St Mary's Church Hall Association, with the Leitrim's Women's Association from the adjoining church, provided plenty of food and drink for all the more mature people who did not wish to attend the pub. The ladies' warmth and hospitality was most appreciated by all those they served and I thanked them most sincerely for the wonderful job they did that day.

Like most occasions when one is under the spotlight or the centre of attention, I didn't know half the people there. Sad times seem to bring out the best in strangers too but all such sympathy was appreciated whatever the source.

It did appear that the entire local community was touched by the sadness of the occasion and it was comforting for all of us affected by the tragedy to see such wonderful people who willingly offered their services voluntary – not only for Kevin's funeral, but also for other people's funerals. It's 'angels' like these who make the pain of grief so much more comforting for those less fortunate during times of trouble and strife. One cannot help but appreciate the work and concern of people like this who ask for nothing in return.

Accompanied by Derry and young Patrick, I made an appearance at both receptions. My mother also called at St Mary's before later joining us at the White Swan.

Despite her obvious distress, Linda and her companions were also present at the White Swan. Although the atmosphere at St Mary's had been generally cordial, back at the pub the scene appeared to be far more sombre and emotive.

I was constantly overwhelmed by sympathisers offering to shake my hand, pay their respects and offer their condolences either by warm embraces, kissing or backslapping. To my utter amazement, I discovered that one of the main talking points was my tribute to Kevin.

So many compliments were paid to me for what was claimed to be one of the best ever speeches (considering the circumstances) that they had ever heard. I will never know how I found the strength that day, but suffice to say that my words certainly not affected just me and my family, but obviously most of the attendees.

The assembly at the White Swan that afternoon and evening included many friends and family from far and wide. In fact, from all over the world.

Hardly surprising and particularly with the funeral arranging which denied me the opportunity to see so many of the sympathisers before the services on both days, this was therefore the perfect opportunity to make amends.

Although it was a long and painfully emotional experience, I walked around for most of the afternoon welcoming and thanking them individually for attending.

I also insisted that those present shouldn't be too morose either. While it was undoubtedly an extremely sad occasion, it was meant to be a happy celebration of Kevin's short life.

I also felt it was appropriate that we should be entertained. At one point I called on one of my great friends, Michael Walker, a Dubliner who has worked in the local area for many years, to give us a song. He obliged by putting in a great performance in true Irish wake tradition that lasted until the early hours of Saturday morning.

It had been suggested several times that afternoon and throughout the evening about doing something in memory of Kevin. Because of his passion for golf as well as the White Swan being so well used to running golf days or supporting golf days for local charities and local people, it was therefore inevitable that an annual Kevin Duggan Golf Day seemed to be appropriate for such a tribute. The first one was arranged for 13th August 1999 to coincide with what would have been his 20th birthday.

However, our celebration of my son's life suddenly took an unexpected turn for the worst when I heard some quite shattering news about the true circumstances of his death

Whilst mingling with some of the sympathisers, I found myself engaged in conversation with a number of Kevin's friends. Anybody familiar with the layout of the White Swan will know that the pool table is located close to the rear door which leads to the beer garden. That corner of the room is also quite close to the door leading to the pub's living quarters.

Shaking hands with Kevin's friends assembled around the pool table, as well as welcoming them into the pub, just seemed like a perfectly natural thing to do. I could detect that emotions were running high with a number of the boys, and many of them had consumed a fair volume of alcohol in the aftermath of the funeral.

But, I was astounded when I discovered that their topic of conversation was, quite unbelievably, the circumstances that led to Kevin's death on that previous Saturday evening.

On overhearing some of this conversation adjacent to the pool table, I was immediately drawn into it like a magnet. The boys were actually comparing each other's accounts of what they had heard - either reliably or through rumour - about how driver Paul Mason and surviving passenger Paul Anstey had spent that Saturday on a day-long pub crawl.

Although gripped by the advanced stages of stress and grief, not to mention the early effects of alcohol and onset of fatigue, I could barely believe what I was hearing – especially after being given a completely different account by the crash investigator, PC Tony Whinnett a couple of days earlier. I still find it hard to differentiate to this very day, which gave me the more sickening feeling on that awful week of my life: learning that my teenage son had been killed in a road crash or being told a blatant lie by the local police that my son WAS NOT the victim of an alcohol-related car crash.

Not alone was the car crash a drink-driving incident, it was also a drink-fuelled crash that even involved a police chase! Almost immediately I realised that grief counselling was not my only priority as I began my quest to find answers to several unexplained questions.

From the delay in actually notifying Kevin's next of kin i.e. between the time of the crash at 10.30 p.m. on Saturday evening until 3.00 a.m. Sunday morning, when my brother Liam was told of the tragedy, to the initial denial by PC Whinnett, the whole case was beginning to look quite baffling.

I am indebted to Kevin's close friend, Paul Clayton, and his friends for being so forthright and responsible in feeling that it was their duty to inform me about what really happened on Saturday 31st October.

It was certainly not the kind of climax to the celebration of my son's life that I had been anticipating, and not surprisingly, once the initial shock of the revelation had worn off, my grief was replaced by extreme anger. Paul Clayton was adamant that driver Paul Mason would not only have been over the limit at the time of the crash but he would also have been "pissed out of his brains!" Clayton's account was later confirmed by PC Coneely, the police officer who had been first to arrive at the scene of the crash.

I could scarcely contain my anger when I heard Clayton's true account surrounding the circumstances of the crash. As I began to tremble with rage, I felt my blood boiling within my veins, not understanding at all why the police seemingly wanted to mislead me so much.

Something sinister was afoot and I was determined to uncover whatever that was. For me, it wasn't hard to see how external forces were already in operation to conceal the true circumstances of the crash.

It was even later disclosed that Philip Mason (the father of the driver) actually contacted his broker, who was representing the insurance company Norwich Union, as soon as he learnt of the crash just before midnight that evening. That seemed somewhat unusual for a man in his situation, who was still unaware whether or not his son was even going to survive the crash.

One could smell a rat alright, but this was a smell that was extremely pungent, if not completely odious or obnoxious. I was determined not to be muzzled, not matter who may have been affected by the consequences. I felt at the very least I owed Kevin justice. The man responsible for my son's death must be brought to book, charged and convicted.

There was certainly no time for one to feel sorry for oneself and whilst I may have been having virtual hallucinations and feeling often somewhat detached from reality, this was the kind of news that soon brought you back to Earth with a bang.

I was determined to act immediately upon this 'hot' confidential information, but I still had the problem about not knowing where to start. I was literally left in a dilemma, not knowing which way to turn.

"Where do I go from here?" I kept asking myself over and over again. I was unsure who I could speak too now that I had lost trust and confidence in the local police force.

*

Not long after the funeral, I had a surprise visit from the parish priest, whom I must confess I really didn't know that well at the time. Despite my good upbringing and whilst I uphold some very strong Christian beliefs, I am not a very religious person and I was somewhat of a lapsed Catholic. Nevertheless, Fr. Quinn felt obliged through his Christian nature, just as much as being part of his pastoral duties, to pay me a visit in order to see how I was coping.

I admitted I felt anything but well during this period, but I still sincerely thanked him for his concern and for all that he did to make the service such a fitting finale for Kevin. He confessed that he had never witnessed an event like that in all the other parishes in which he had served. I replied that I wished it had not been necessary for me to do so, but I also thanked God for giving me the strength and inspiration to face the congregation.

Likewise, on discovering that I had been seriously misinformed by the local police, I was equally inspired to do everything in my power to get justice for Kevin. This personal objective had now been thrust upon me and became my main priority in life during the aftermath of his tragic death.

That week of the funeral was certainly a low point in my life but now, even that awful week, was being superseded by a far worst feeling inside me: a feeling of sheer utter betrayal had now become another unwelcome component of my grieving process as I tried to come to terms with the consequences of receiving the so far unexplained false information from the local police.

There were some damning questions which required immediate answers, such as:

- Who was being giving this false information and what were the reasons for it?

- Who was being protected by this misinformation?

These questions just wouldn't go away. They played on my mind over and over again.

I needed to get to the bottom of them and I was determined to do just that, whatever it took. I looked for the same kind of inspiration which had given me such strength throughout the funeral service.

Unfortunately, like most grieving parents who would now have been able to get on with the rest of their lives, my problems were only just beginning. However, after the tremendous display of sympathy I had received throughout the funeral, I knew I wouldn't lack any support as I began my campaign for justice and the uncovering of the truth of what had actually happened to my son.

Chapter Nine

Just how were the police going to explain their awful lie from that previous Sunday?

Still reeling from Paul Clayton's revelation in the White Swan on 5th November, the evening of the wake, I didn't hesitate in getting some kind of game plan into action in order to uncover the true facts about what had happened. Not surprisingly, the local police were in no hurry about coming forward and offering any kind of explanation.

In fact, with the exception of PC Chris Coneely, quite a number of the local force did anything but cover themselves in glory in the days following the tragedy. However, it was still too soon to suspect that anything sinister resembling a blatant 'cover-up' of the facts surrounding the crash was in hand.

During the course of the investigation over the next 12 months, it was discovered that there may have been an attempt to distort the true facts, even before my brother Liam was informed of Kevin's death at 3.00 a.m. on Sunday 1st November

Despite my distress and anger on realising that I still wouldn't be allowed to grief and mourn my son's death while all these nagging doubts about the course of the crash remained unexplained, I felt comforted by the concern of my customers and I was also inspired by Fr. Quinn's visit after the funeral (who said he would pray for me and offered me the advice that I needed to pick myself up, dust myself down and start all over again – safe words indeed).

I was determined to speak to investigating officer PC Tony Whinnett as soon as possible. Not surprisingly, that proved to be much easier said than done. Almost two weeks had elapsed since the funeral but for one reason or another, PC Whinnett was not available, either because he was on duty or on leave. I was convinced I was being given the run about in my quest to obtain answers to some very serious questions.

Whilst I have been writing this book, a young man called Mark Duggan (no relation) had been shot by police one evening in August 2011. Because of my own experience, I feel I am qualified to comment not just on the shooting but the police response to inform the family after Mark's unfortunate death.

Mark Duggan was shot dead by a police marksman at approx 6.15 p.m. on 4th August 2011. There is a lot of speculation as to what happened that evening but that isn't for me to discuss amongst these pages and I'm sure the debate will rage on for a number of years yet.

Personally what I feel is important, and brings back memories of anger and frustration, is the aftermath of what happened and how the police dealt with informing the family that their loved one had been killed.

Duggan was a family man with three young children and was engaged to be married. He was shot by a single bullet through the chest and although attended quite quickly by a medical team, he was pronounced dead at the scene.

Not only was there confusion and speculation surrounding the fatal shooting but worse was yet to come as who was to be actually responsible for informing Mark's family about what had happened?

The void of any information being relayed to Mark's family or next of kin was the main issue that sparked the worst scenes of violence, rioting, looting and arson that London had ever witnessed since World War Two when the city was bombed by the Luftwaffe.

Even two days later (6th August), the family still not had any contact from the police or anyone else in authority. There was no other choice: the Duggan family, relatives and friends marched from the Broadwater Farm Estate[24] to Tottenham Police Station.

There they demanded to know why and how Mark Duggan was killed and why no one had contacted them with any explanation as to the shooting and why was there now nothing but complete silence?

---

[24] A council housing estate in Tottenham, North London, notorious for a mid-1980s riot.

The lack of any response from the police, not just as a professional public body, but as a civic duty – surely they should have been speaking to the family who were now suffering a huge loss in grieving for their son?

The protest outside the police station quickly became very tense as many hundreds were now turning up to the vigil. The mood of the crowd turned angry and at about 8.00 p.m., a 16-year-old girl was hurt in a clash with the police. The crowd retaliated and turned on the police with two police cars being set alight. This was the start of what was to become the worst disorder and violence seen in the country for decades – first in London, before spreading to other cities throughout the UK[25].

Why on earth didn't the police contact the Duggan family?

Where were the police family liaison officers?

Where were the social services – after all, there were three young children now involved as their father had been shot dead?

Where were the local councillors? The local community leaders? The local MP?

Why didn't the police come clean, open up and tell the truth? Why did they distort the truth and blame the victim for shooting at them first?

Obviously, the best form of defence for the police was to stay silent, admit nothing, get the story right and then cover up where they could.

In my opinion, what they should have done within hours of what had happened, was for the highest ranking officer or Commander or Chief Superintendent, along with the police family liaison officer, to visit Mark's wife and children and tell them the bad news. Of course this would have been a tough decision to make at the time but it was the only sensible way through what was the most difficult of situations.

---

[25] Between 6th and 10th August 2011, rioting broke out in several London boroughs which then spread across various towns and cities. Thousands took to the streets causing widespread rioting looting and arson.

During heartbreaking and sad times, especially when losing a loving family member, you need to hear the truth, the whole truth and nothing but the truth. More importantly, you need to hear it without delay, no matter what the circumstances are. Not only should justice be done, it must be seen to be done.

The police are there to protect, serve and uphold the law, not just to build a wall of silence and then conspire to cover up the true facts of any crime.

Mark Duggan's family condemned any violence that followed his fatal shooting and subsequently the police did apologise to them for not communicating in a proper and sympathetic way.

*

While I was waiting for my much anticipated showdown with PC Whinnett, I had a surprise telephone call from another police officer who just happened to be in the vicinity of the scene of the road crash. It was PC Chris Coneely requesting to meet him near the White Swan.

Was this the hand of fate about to intervene and expose the lies of PC Coneely's own colleagues?

Coneely was one of three policeman brothers from a well-known Irish family in the Luton and Dunstable area and apart from being the first officer at the scene, he appeared so determined to disclose to me the true facts and emphasised how much alcohol was responsible for Kevin's death.

We arranged to meet one evening while he was off duty at the rear of the White Swan, away from the public glare. I often wonder why he agreed to do this and can only put it down to the fact that both our fathers had known each other and that the sense of family, and what was right, of honour, was important to both our families.

After a few follow-up telephone conversations with PC Coneely and still no contact from PC Whinnett, I was now beginning to lose faith in the local constabulary, and although I was now becoming angrier, bitter and more frustrated by the day, I was still determined to maintain my composure.

I decided to also contact my local councillor and former Mayor, Cllr. Bill Stephens, who advised me to speak to local Chief Superintendent Brian Minahane. I also enlisted the help of my licensing officer PC Ian Farrow in another attempt to make a breakthrough.

PC Whinnett did make contact eventually, in early December, but instead of inviting me to the police station in Dunstable, he suggested he pay me a visit in Luton instead.

Accompanied by a Sergeant with reams of paperwork in his arms, PC Whinnett arrived for what had now become a long overdue meeting. However, I had to conceal my frustration because I knew I had to tread delicately in my questioning.

PC Whinnett's opening gambit was more related to explaining police procedure in dealing with all kinds of fatalities no matter what the cause may be. Despite my anger level almost at boiling point, I wasn't going to be sidetracked and demanded to know why my family was being so blatantly misinformed in relation to the facts of the crash.

To his credit, PC Whinnett did apologise, but insisted that the police were quite in order to withhold any information that might cause even more distress to relatives of the deceased at the time of the tragedy. I countered by arguing that this was a very unprofessional approach by the police and asked when did they think was the correct time to reveal the truth? Was this going to be days, weeks, months or perhaps even not at all?

While I was relieved that PC Whinnett and his colleague had taken the time to meet with me and offer their explanation, I was far from satisfied and had no confidence in their ability to conduct the investigation into the cause of the crash. I also made my feelings known later to Cllr. Stephens, who suggested that the both of us should go and see Chief Superintendent Minahane early in the New Year.

My other priority was now to get my own investigation underway to uncover as much information as I could about the circumstances that led to the tragedy. If I could not rely on the local police to uncover the whole truth, then the obvious course of action left for me was to either do it myself or enlist the help of some friends to undertake our own investigation work.

Believe it or not, my starting point began in the most unlikely of sources, a conversation with one of my customers from the White Swan.

*

Phil 'The Suit' Maule is a colourful character, well known to the regulars of the White Swan and was later to become one of the most pivotal members in a small campaign group that can proudly claim so much credit for both securing a conviction for drink-drive suspect Paul Mason, as well as the introduction of landmark legislation to blood test unconscious drink-drive suspects in October 2002, namely 'Duggan's Law'.

Maule was quite familiar with the effects of excessive alcohol consumption and it had even been claimed that he was an alcoholic. It may have seemed a strange starting point for me to tackle such a gargantuan undertaking and after some initial rebuttals, I eventually relented early in 1999.

During midweek on a cold wet January evening and still feeling in the depths of despair, I was left with no other alternative but to agree with Maule to put a plan of action into place without further delay. It looked a hopeless task, having to rely on a man that at the time I knew very little about but has now, in retrospect, proved to be one of my most inspired decisions.

Always one of our more smartly dressed customers and hence the nickname 'The Suit', Maule was also very astute and an intelligent individual until too much alcohol got the better of him and the 'wheels fell off'.

However, Phil also had miraculous recovery qualities. Sadly there were also moments, just like the rest of us, when he could even make a slight fool of himself, but to his many dear friends he was generally an impeccably behaved human being.

My initial meeting with Phil certainly proved to be one of the most defining moments of my life because that occasion proved to be so instrumental in formulating the overall strategy we adopted and which led to such a successful conclusion.

Another reason why Phil's role proved so crucial was his own personal affinity with Kevin. He therefore had no hesitation in offering his services in whatever way he could help.

Despite the fact that he had a past drink-drive conviction, I was still confident in Phil's capability and aptitude for the task ahead. He led our private investigation effort to uncover the facts that the police were either not interested in detecting or simply appeared to not want to know.

Phil worked tirelessly gathering all the relevant intelligence and information from wherever it was possible and perhaps his most valuable contribution to the campaign group was his very effective and skilful recording of information, either on computer disc or in written note form. Much of that information included copious minutes from the numerous meetings we attended over the next four years.

There were also times when I wondered how he was so efficient in gathering all this relevant information. Although he failed to disclose it early in his investigation work, I discovered some months into the campaign that he once worked as an investigator for legal and insurance companies.

Phil's lighter side included some very funny moments surrounding his drinking lifestyle which always amused us. I can vividly remember one particular occasion in the White Swan, whilst steep in conversation about events that took place earlier that day, still feeling the worse for wear, he suddenly slipped off his seat and under the table. But he immediately reappeared again to take his place and resume his conversation as if nothing had happened!

Still pretending to feel unruffled in any way, he questioned what was so amusing to cause such a widespread outburst of laughter. His unpredictable behaviour may have been his Achilles heel, but it was always sure to entertain no matter how serious the circumstances might be.

But, for his faults and brushes with the demon drink, Phil was always a very sharp and intelligent individual. He had an amazing photographic memory with the ability to recall facts many weeks previously and was therefore able to reveal them at the most appropriate times.

Unlike many individuals who lost their memory as a result of excessive drinking, Phil's memory appeared to be completely unaffected. On a number of occasions following late night drinking sessions, he was always capable of recalling every last detail of conversations from that previous evening.

In early January, I had also acquired the support of the local press as well as our local MP. I was determined to express my deep dissatisfaction with the conduct of certain members of the local police service, which was why I arranged to meet Margaret Moran MP that previous December.

Similar to my introduction to 'Phil The Suit', my meeting with Luton South MP Margaret Moran at her surgery in Union Street, Luton was also the beginning of what has now become a wonderfully productive professional association.

In a room occupied by up to 30 or so of her constituents, I was the last in line to see her. Although she looked quite tired, Margaret, on hearing the serious nature of my story, expressed real concern about my problem with the local police and their investigation of the fatal crash. As well as taking notes in the course of our conversation, Margaret also asked local photographer Gareth Owen to take our picture because in her words, "We've got a lot of work to do."

I cannot be certain where the photograph was published but it was not long before the local press were taking a serious interest in our campaign. The Herald & Post were represented by an aspiring young reporter by the name of Gill Harris, who was later also to become an integral and final part of our small campaign committee.

But, before we began our own enquiries, Cllr. Stephens and I decided to meet with Chief Superintendent Brian Minahane in the New Year. I was hoping that he would provide the answers to many of my questions.

Yet, my meeting with the Chief Superintendant was far from satisfactory because I felt I was not being taken very seriously by what I considered was a very aloof individual. I went to the police station in Dunstable searching for answers and all I received was a succession of stilted replies including his own remark that a death on the road was just like any other cause of death, including murder, and would therefore be investigated accordingly.

I remember looking over at Cllr. Stephens more than once during the conversation and could see that he was also of the same opinion; we were getting nowhere fast.

Whilst I felt like telling the Superintendent what I thought of him and his replies, I thought better of it, brought the discussion to an end by asking him why I had not been told the full facts surrounding the tragedy and why was I being forced to uncover these facts by my own resource.

Minahane replied that all the relevant enquiries would be carried out in good time. The police procedures could not be rushed, not to mention the 'manpower' factor which was also slowing down the enquiries. It was so frustrating having to listen to his feel and far from genuine excuses.

I finally snapped as I stood up from my chair to leave the room saying, "You don't know what it feels like to be sitting this side of the table." What I mean by that was why were we not getting the answers to the questions we were asking and in particular why had there been no reference made to the fact that alcohol had made such a significant contribution to Kevin's death?

Eventually, Minahane replied, "I can assure you Mr. Duggan, you will get all the answers and a full investigation will be carried out in good time."

Unfortunately, I knew this to be a hollow promise. I bit my lip and walked out of the door to begin what would now become a parallel investigation into the circumstances of my teenage son's death.

Since the police investigation into the cause of the tragedy was proving to be so unreliable, our small campaign group had no alternative other than to both support and monitor the work of the local police force.

Declan with son Kevin

Kevin

Declan at
Stockwood Park Greens

The Duggan family, with a young Kevin

Declan with the Professional Golfers' Association's Chief Executive Sandy Jones and the Ryder Cup

Margaret Moran, David Blunkett MP and Kevin Whately with the Ryder Cup

Declan at The Kevin Duggan Golf
Academy

Declan

Declan and Irish PM
Enda Kenny

Declan behind the bar at his pub
The White Swan with Kevin Whately

Kevin with Kerrie and Roisin

Declan with wife Derry and children Patrick, Danny and Sinead
with Danny Fitzsimmons

Kevin Whately with Declan's staff, sisters Elle and Molly, Corinne,
and daughters Roisin and Sinead

Chapter Ten

Following my unsatisfactory meeting with Chief Superintendent Brian Minahane, my next objective was to meet investigating officer PC Tony Whinnett. However, unlike the co-operation I received from prime crash witness PC Chris Coneely, PC Whinnett was proving to be rather elusive.

I also attempted to liaise with PC Whinnett through my local licensing officer PC Ian Farrow, but any time he attempted to make enquiries on my behalf, he was politely informed by his superiors that it was none of his business.

Eventually, after constant badgering, PC Whinnett did accede to my request and came to my home in Luton for the first in a number of meetings briefing me on the progress of the crash investigation.

Accompanied by a police sergeant with reams of paperwork, I was almost at saturation point with frustration and rage as I patiently listened to them making excuse after excuse for their lack of progress with the investigation. All I wanted to know was why was my family and I were being treated so poorly and receiving such unreliable information about the facts of the tragedy.

PC Whinnett was completely a different individual in comparison to the man I first met at the Luton & Dunstable Hospital when I formally identified Kevin. There, he had been vague about things but now he was understanding and caring, though still somehow unwilling to provide answers to any of my questions. His body language also didn't seem right and I was determined to find out why this was.

When I asked him to explain the unreliability of their information he firstly apologised but then added that there were various ways the police dealt with grieving parents' feelings and that there were certain times that information had to be held back and released slowly.

I vigorously challenged this feeble explanation and even suggested that it was unprofessional of the police service to treat grieving relatives in such a patronising way. Almost losing my temper with the both of them, I made it crystal clear that I wanted to know the truth now and not weeks or months later.

PC Whinnett eventually admitted that driver Paul Mason was being uncooperative with the police and their enquiries and also that his parents were also doing a very effective job in shielding him from the law. And that was about all the information I obtained from the meeting. To be expected, I wasn't satisfied, not in the least.

PC Coneely's involvement and assistance in our investigation cannot be overstated on the other hand. Had he not come forward to reveal the full facts in such a covert way, we may have never been any of the wiser. Perhaps this is what PC Whinnett and some of his other colleagues wanted...I guess I will never know for certain[26].

I can never forget the frustration I suffered those early months of 1999. Were it not for the support of my colleagues in the campaign group, my family and great friends, I just don't know what I would have done while I waited and wondered to see if the police force were going to act against the driver who was responsible for killing my son.

The procrastination by some members of the local police service in bringing charges against Mason were now more than obvious. I knew and felt there were some other factor (or factors) obstructing the course of justice that was, at that time, still unknown to me.

It felt like I was now policing the police themselves.

Working in conjunction with the campaign group members (Phil Maule, Gill Harris and Margaret Moran MP), it was clear we needed a firm game plan if we were going to get the kind of results we needed to convince the police that driver Mason should be held to account in some way for the carnage he had caused that Saturday October 31st 1998.

Despite encountering all the obvious distractions and obstructions from whatever source they may have been, I never allowed my weak

---

[26] ...which is sadly true even to this day.

emotional state and broken heart to affect the campaign group's work in any way. My determination and unquenchable spirit ensured that I had absolutely no fear in tackling the authorities by just simply asking:

"How was my son killed? Why was my son killed? Why are my family and I being treated in such an appalling way?"

*

Following my pre-Christmas meeting with Margaret Moran MP, her first reaction in dealing with my serious problems was to arrange a meeting with the then Road Safety Minister, Lord (Larry) Whitty[27] and his various civil servants and advisors.

It was imperative also that a number of road safety groups be contacted to see if we could gain some support in our quest to find out why it was only Kevin's blood which was tested at the hospital following the crash.

Because both Mason and Anstey were unconscious and therefore unable to offer their consent, neither gave blood samples at the scene of the crash or at the hospital.

That was when I first discovered that driver Mason could not face drink-drive charges due to lack of evidence.

On Friday 14th July, Phil Maule and I travelled to Westminster in order to meet Margaret Moran and her Labour party colleague and former trade union official Lord Whitty.

Steeped in history and tradition, one could not but be impressed with a visit to Parliament, but sadly that was about all that was memorable from our first visit to Westminster.

We were invited into a committee room and sat around a large table. There we were soon joined by Lord Whitty and his support staff of advisors and civil servants.

---

[27] Baron Whitty PC (born John Lawrence Whitty; 15th June 1943 -); Labour politician; employed by Trades Union Congress (1970 – 1973) and General Municipal Boilermakers and Allied Trade Union (1973 – 1985); General Secretary of the Labour Party (1985 – 1994); European Coordinator for Labour (1994 – 1997). Made life peer in 1996.

Margaret opened the discussion and gave a brief summary of the situation thus far and that we were trying to achieve a possible travesty of justice due to some legal loophole on blood testing drink-drive suspects, as well as the progress of the police investigation into the causes of the tragedy.

Our main objective was to establish why the blood samples of the person who caused the crash and the other unconscious passenger weren't taken and yet somebody was able to take a sample of my dead son's blood without any kind of consent from his next of kin.

I found it absolutely ridiculous that the most relevant blood test of all, namely that of the driver, had somehow been protected by what was then a serious loophole. As it happened, Kevin's blood test was in fact well below the legal alcohol limit.

Sadly, as I glanced across at Lord Whitty, it became obvious that our pleas for help were falling on deaf ears. As I began to speak, I even noticed him taking a sneak peak at his watch. I began to ask myself privately what we were doing there as he was not listening to a word I was saying.

Margaret Moran was also far from impressed with her colleague's disinterest, not to mention his crass behaviour towards us. We were hoping our visit was going to offer us some kind of hope, but the outcome of this meeting was certainly not the kind of start to our campaign that we had in mind. When we left the meeting, we were severely disappointed.

But since a consultation with Lord Whitty was not going to be the answer to our problems, we had no other alternative but to bypass him and call on the assistance of the Great Lady of the House, Gwyneth Dunwoody MP[28], who was then the Chairman of the Transport Select Committee.

---

[28] Gwyneth Dunwoody (12th December 1930 – 17th April 2008); Labour politician; represented Exeter (1966 – 1970); Crewe (then Crewe and Nantwich) from 1974 until her death.

Margaret subsequently arranged the campaign group's next visit to Westminster which was scheduled for later that year.

*

The campaign group's other investigation work concentrated on developments much closer to home with reporter Gill Harris ensuring that our progress was never kept out of the local newspapers.

Phil Maule continued to make some discreet enquiries which included a visit to all four pubs in Dunstable where Mason and Anstey had drunk on the day of the tragedy. He was greeted with a wall of silence in all but one of the pubs. The landlady of the Winston Churchill was quite willing to assist and confirmed that both Mason and Anstey began their drinking spree at 11.00 a.m. where they both consumed three pints each.

Perhaps one of the most interesting developments in the campaign group's investigation occurred on the day that Anstey was discharged from hospital, just a few weeks before Christmas.

Despite colluding with Mason by distorting the facts during the aftermath of the crash, Anstey – who was still on crutches – was summarily dismissed from his job with Three Counties Scaffolding that same day. This company was owned by Paul Mason's father, Phillip.

Without hesitation, Anstey immediately got into a taxi and headed to the White Swan, in order to break the news to me about this unbelievably poor treatment by his employer.

I remember meeting Anstey as he got out of the taxi and saying something like, "Declan, I have something to tell you and I don't know whether you're going to like what you're about to hear."

I replied by saying that any kind of news was welcome as long as it wasn't more bad news. Anstey couldn't really be blamed for being coerced into siding with the Masons after the crash, but in the end they paid dearly for their cruel, heartless humiliation and betray of him the day he was discharged from hospital.

Anstey had some quite disturbing information about what the Masons were planning to do in their attempt to prevent their son facing justice. This information would also prove to be most interesting to the police enquiries.

He knew also that the Masons were the first next of kin to be informed after the crash and he was also aware of the late night telephone call made by the insurance broker to Norwich Union. Anstey believed finally that the Masons had alleged Freemason connections. Phil Maule later confirmed that this may have been the case.

Paul Mason is said to have been too ill to help the police with their enquiries while he was in hospital and with Anstey's statement denying any kind of alcohol involvement on the night of the crash, the Masons were adamant their son would evade any kind of police interview for as long as they possibly could.

Reports from my two daughters, Kerrie and Roisin, that Mason had been driving around Dunstable in a brand new Ford Mondeo 1.6 were confirmed one day in March as I stood and watched in horror on the doorstep of the White Swan. While the police were briefing me about their supposed failure to interview a dangerous driving suspect, it was plain to see he was perfectly fit to drive around the roads of Dunstable without a care in the world!

I had no hesitation in telling the police what I had seen so how was he continuing to evade their questioning? I received yet another frustrating reply that as far as the law was concerned, he had committed no crime and thus he was innocent until proven guilty.

My response was that Mason was a convicted drink-driver who was responsible for killing my son and I'll admit, I concluded the conversation by screaming down the telephone asking what more evidence they needed to put this kid and his irresponsible father on trial for causing death by dangerous driving?

The contribution of PC Coneely at this stage also proved decisive, and even his superiors PC Whinnett and other members of the Traffic Division had by now realised that they would have to do a humiliating, if not embarrassing, U-turn from their previous stance in the case. Coneely's crucial evidence from the scene of the crash had now become common knowledge and it was only a matter of time before Paul Mason finally would be getting his collar felt.

Despite Mason's "What have I done to be guilty?" attitude, the police did eventually close in on him about a month or so later. Accompanied by his father, his solicitor (who was also representing Norwich Union, their insurance company), Mason was finally questioned by Dunstable police and charged with causing death by dangerous driving in May.

Mason and his parents were still being as uncooperative as they could. They even had the gall to argue the validity of why their son was being questioned or even under suspicion in the first place, and why should he be facing any kind of prosecution.

It is believed that Mason caused quite an unpleasant scene whilst under investigation and continued to protest his innocence throughout his interrogation by detectives. His complete denial of any wrongdoing was yet another blatant 'kick-in-the-teeth' for our campaign and for me personally, the real victim of the tragedy.

But, those who were attempting to pervert the course of justice from whatever society they belonged to, secret or otherwise, were also powerless to prevent the system finally taking its full course, almost 12 months after Kevin's death.

Many of my supporters, including members of the campaign group – who had been quite apprehensive during those early stages about securing a successful completion – were now much more optimistic about the prospects of success.

Our determination and persistence finally paid off when Mason was charged and hopefully there could now only be one outcome as the countdown to Mason's appearance in court, on 11th October, began to gather momentum.

Part of the preparation for our day in court included securing the help of Roger Ball from the Victim's Support Group. Roger arranged for us to be briefed on court procedures on all the rules of evidence including the distinction between what was 'admissible' and 'inadmissible'. These meetings took place with both the Crown Prosecution Service (CPS) and also the Prosecution barristers.

They were all horrified to hear the full facts of the case, but when it came to the legal representatives and Roger explaining the judicial system, most of us were enraged to discover that unless we had cast iron proof that driver Mason was drinking, then we would not succeed in any charge of drink-driving.

At the time my immediate reaction was why was there so much disparity between the rights of the victims compared to the perpetrators of crime?

However, all our frustrations resulting from the weakness of the judicial system were completely overshadowed by the determination of our group to secure a conviction. We knew we had a fight on our hands, but now we had that chance we were not going to waste it.

Meanwhile, Margaret Moran was briefing Phil and I for our return to Westminster in June for our much anticipated meeting with the Chairman of the Transport Select Committee, Gwyneth Dunwoody MP. Since we now enjoyed the real prospect of securing a conviction in court, much had now changed since our disappointing earlier meeting with Lord Whitty in January.

Our meeting with her could not have been in more contrast. It was a bright sunny day and we began by giving her all our available information.

Margaret had described her as a no-nonsense type and then having met her, I certainly agree. When it came for her turn to speak, she got straight to the point.

During my presentation of the case, she interrupted a number of times to ask questions. She had an in-depth knowledge of why we were there and what we were trying to achieve: a change in the law that prevented unconscious drink-drive suspects from being blood tested at the scene of a crash.

She listened attentively before giving Margaret and myself all the correct guidelines and briefed us on the process of the way forward if we were going achieve our goals.

Gwyneth Dunwoody can certainly claim to have paved the way for Margaret and I by giving us a list of things and what to do and how to do it as well as who to go and speak too.

Having had the door almost slammed in our faces only six months previously, it now appeared to be very much ajar and the onus was on us to open it as wide as we possibly could over the ensuing months. She also advised that the next step (amongst a series of steps) was to arrange a meeting with one of her close colleagues, Charles Clarke MP[29].

After this very productive meeting, Margaret, Phil and I headed to St Pancras Station to catch the train back to Luton.

On the train we formulised our game plan including the delegation of who was doing what before we met up with our fourth campaign member, Gill Harris, back at the White Swan.

Without a doubt, our meeting with Gwyneth Dunwoody was certainly another defining moment in the campaign. After six months we had our first serious breakthrough and therefore we felt quite justified in celebrating the occasion.

Between that moment and the October court date was arguably the most important period of the whole campaign, which kept every member of the group focused on one task or another.

And, besides co-ordinating the organisation of the first annual Kevin Duggan Golf Day on what would have been his twentieth birthday in August, Derry and I got married in September.

But, all these exciting events in my life, as well as contemplating any change in the drink-drive law were well down the pecking order of the campaign group's immediate objective, namely that of securing the conviction of Paul Mason at his trial, which began on 11th October 1999.

---

[29] Charles Clarke (21st September 1950 -); Labour politician; represented Norwich South (1997 – 2010); Home Secretary (December 2004 – May 2006).

Declan Duggan

Chapter Eleven

The trial at Luton Crown Court was expected to last a week. Commencing Monday 11th October 1999, much of the trial procedure proved to be no more than a rehash or even a regurgitation of the evidence gathered by the police, supported by our campaign group.

As in most criminal proceedings, the trial involved listening to the evidence provided by the counsel for the defence and then the counsel representing the Criminal Prosecution Service (CPS). Evidence was available through a number of appearing witnesses and video recordings.

I was quite fortunate in having the benefit of knowing what to expect amidst the anticipated courtroom drama, not to mention what evidence was admissible or inadmissible. For much of my preparatory work ahead of the trial, I was very much indebted to Roger Ball of the Victim Support Group.

Roger's advice was meticulous and ranged from where the prosecution and victim's relatives would likely to be sitting, to where the representatives of the accused could be positioned.

The proximity of the two parties were never too close or where even eye contact could be established. However, despite Roger's advice, I couldn't help myself from attempting to gauge the mood of Paul Mason's supporters.

In keeping with his undeniable display of remorseless, blatantly ignoring the serious nature of the charges he was facing, I also couldn't believe that Mason's parents were acting with seemingly carefree banter, punctuated even by the odd joke or shriek of laughter.

Their upbeat mood seemed to reflect a misguided belief and optimism that their son's ordeal would soon be over and that he would be acquitted.

Accompanied by his father, mother, sister and some of his friends, Paul Mason refused to accept any responsibility for the tragedy that fateful evening in October 1998. His cold, heartless and even callous stance left me speechless and stone-faced. But this despicable attitude made me more determined that he should be brought to book for his crime.

Throughout, I never attempted to make eye contact with him, even if I was struggling desperately to contain my own internal rage. I dared not give him the satisfaction of publicly displaying my own private feelings.

I remained cool, calm and collected, despite all the distraction created by our opponents' graceless behaviour. I refused to allow my composure to be affected in any way. And, though the Masons appeared hopeful of securing an acquittal, I was always confident justice would prevail.

The trial began with the customary swearing in of the judge and jury. The jury were then asked to briefly leave the courtroom while both counsels set down their legal arguments and agreed the rules of evidence, particularly what was admissible and what was not.

To my utter dismay, not to mention the frustration of the prosecution counsel, we then discovered that the courtroom would not be allowed to hear how the boys had spent that Saturday before the crash at 10.30 p.m.

There was to be no reference whatsoever to the day-long pub crawl in Dunstable, nor any mention to where they had been before the crash on the Tring Road. I could scarcely contain myself and felt like interrupting proceedings several times.

I believed the jury were entitled to know all the evidence and needed to see the full picture as opposed to the very obvious imbalanced view they were now likely to receive.

But, just as the other frustrated members of the prosecution, I sat, listened, bit my lip and kept quiet. If I didn't, I risked being charged with being contempt of court and faced the ignominy of being physically ejected.

The only matter left resolved by both counsels was what charge, or charges, Mason would face in this particular trial. This was perhaps the most significant part I personally played in the entire proceedings.

As I was clearly a victim of Paul Mason's crime, I was entitled to be consulted about the type of charge he should face, which I would find acceptable. My first consideration was whether or not I would accept a charge of careless driving instead of causing death by dangerous driving.

I refused to accept anything less than the latter charge. In addition to this, Mason also faced the prospect of being charged with failing to stop.

Certainly, I was in no mood to make any kind of concession because all the evidence was in place to secure a conviction – which even the police were now chasing!!! How times had changed.

Even if it couldn't be proved that Mason was over the legal alcohol limit, there was sufficient evidence to prove that he was driving at over 80 miles per hour in the most hazardous of conditions, pursued by a police car before finally colliding with a tree and killing my son. If that wasn't grounds for causing death by dangerous driving, then I wasn't sure what was.

Proceedings began with the prosecution (CPS) presenting their case, which also included PC Tony Whinnett taking the stand to give his own account. Much of the other evidence was provided by computer and video link.

A very impressive presentation was concluded by a complete re-enactment of the journey the three boys made after leaving the Hungry Horse pub, although they were not allowed to mention that was their departure point during the evidence. Apart from victims of the crime not then being permitted to give evidence and make depositions, I felt the prosecution case could not have been presented more thorough than it was.

As an aside, I have now been reliably informed by Margaret Moran MP that the victims of serious crime, including murder, may now be permitted to make what is known as a victim impact statement. A well-known example of this was delivered by Elizabeth Davidson (from Hamilton, Scotland) who lost her 26-year-old daughter, Margaret, in a road crash in Kidlington, Oxon, in May 2006. Margaret, who was a doctor at Horton Hospital, was killed instantly by teenage driver Nolan Haworth as she sat in her stationary car.

During Haworth's sentencing at his trial in September 2007, Judge Julian Hall was reduced to tears when Elizabeth read her statement, where she described her daughter as beautiful, fiercely intelligent, caring and thoughtful.

"My heart is broken. While I am devastated she has been taken I would rather suffer this pain than never to have the love we shared in those 26 years. I loved Margaret from her first breath and will love, mourn and miss her until my last," said a tearful Mrs Davidson.

Elizabeth insists however, that her statement had no bearing on the four year sentence handed down to Haworth, and although I was not afforded a similar opportunity to voice the extent of my loss, I too agree with her that very few judges would be prepared to order the maximum sentence of 14 years imprisonment for such a crime.

Nevertheless, despite not having the chance to make such a statement, I was still hopeful of a positive outcome from the trial. I was also quite confident before the defence began their presentation, that the CPS had done everything possible to secure the conviction. But, I also knew that we had a big fight on our hands.

The main defence argument throughout the trial was the road conditions on that particular evening. It was an exceptionally wet evening for sure, but hardly mitigating circumstances for driving recklessly or irresponsibly even whilst being pursued by the police.

Mason's defence were going to find it extremely difficult justifying his speed when he did finally impact with the tree, however they were trying to spin it. Sadly, but I suppose somewhat understandably, the defence counsel tried every trick in the book rather than admit that their client was responsible.

Witnesses (who had been near to the scene of the tragedy) were drafted in to corroborate just how bad the weather was that evening. The defence counsel certainly left no stone unturned and displayed no lack of imagination in their attempts to get Mason off the hook.

Trying to detach myself from the proceedings, I just couldn't understand why the members of the defence counsel weren't able to see through the seemingly tenuous and suspect integrity of their client. Whatever they were briefed about Mason, they surely must have realised that with such a poor previous record and serious antecedents, including convictions for drink-driving and speeding, the spoilt young thug had very little going for him as he took to the stand.

How people can find it in their hearts to defend the indefensible is also well beyond my comprehension. Right up to the point of judgement or the jury's verdict, Mason never did the decent thing and admitted his responsibility or accepted any blame for the tragedy he caused.

Certainly, if he had shown even the slightest remorse for killing my son, his life might have been so much better afterwards. He also might have been respected in being man enough to look at people like me in the eye. But, his parents too were also far from blameless for the stance they took right throughout the trial.

Even if they were attempting to sway the jury's opinion that they were powerless from preventing their son taking a high powered vehicle out on the public highway and killing somebody, surely they must have known the difference between right and wrong when it came to the time for him to face up and accept the consequences of his crime. As far as I am concerned, the Masons were responsible for encouraging their son's mindless and irresponsible behaviour. It was also painfully evident that their only real objective was to get their 19-year-old boy acquitted, whatever it took.

I have often wondered how I would feel if it was me on the other side of the fence. I know I would have made some attempt to offer an apology of some kind as well as my condolences for their loss due to my own flesh and blood, but even to this day, neither Mason nor a member of his family have come forward and said sorry.

As had been anticipated by Roger Ball, the five day trial certainly did not lack drama but there were several particular key moments which I felt had a huge bearing in the outcome of the court case.

Proceedings were interrupted on the Wednesday. The jury were requested to visit the scene of the crash on the Tring Road. They were directed by the judge to retrace the final steps of the occupants of Mason's car on the route that evening, but not the places they had frequented.

Bearing in mind that this was now very close to the first anniversary of Kevin's death, I decided to go early that particular morning to place two bouquets of flowers by the tree at the crash site. Since his death, I have become quite accustomed to laying flowers on each anniversary of the crash, as well as his birthday and at Christmas.

When the court reconvened the following day I noticed an eerie tension throughout the courtroom. The defence barrister opened proceedings by voicing his disgust on observing the bouquets by the tree. They even wanted the case dismissed because they claimed the flowers were deliberately planted there in order to sway the jury members' opinions.

Apparently Mason's supporters and friends had also visited the crash scene on the Tuesday (when there were no flowers present). I was quite baffled by the defence's line of argument and how they attempted to make what was no more than a tribute or innocent gesture to my late son, appear like an offence.

I guess it was just another example of the depth they were prepared to go to with what was yet another cynical attempt by Mason and his supporters to get him acquitted.

The CPS listened patiently and attentively to the defence counsel's argument before the judge called a halt to the debate and stated that no crime had been committed and that friends and family of the deceased were entitled to place flowers at the scene of a crash whenever they felt appropriate to do so.

Since placing of flowers at the scene of a death was now quite common practice throughout the country, the defence counsel had no foundation whatsoever to make a complaint. Mason's feeble defence was now beginning to feel like it was resting on a wing and a bouquet of flowers!

Watching Paul Mason taking the stand for questioning also proved to be a most frustrating part of the trial. This was mainly because he couldn't be questioned about where he had been earlier that day or evening of the crash.

Prosecution barrister Mr Malik, representing the CPS, then finally summed up his cross-examination of a heartless and completely insensitive Mason by asking him if he felt in any way responsible for the death of his friend Kevin Duggan.

Not surprisingly, Mason's negative reply drew gasps of utter disbelief from the majority of the courtroom. His stance undoubtedly did much to undermine his credibility for the remainder of the trial.

Any decent human being would surely have realised from the moment that he sat behind the wheel until he invited Kevin into the passenger seat of his vehicle that he had some kind of duty of care for him?

But, because Mason chose to deny any responsibility, it was obvious that the trial began to go downhill for him. Although he was asked the same question in a number of different ways, his answer stayed the same: it had nothing to do with him.

And because of this, I felt utter contempt for him, his family and his supporters. It was so hard and painful to observe the way this young man was being advised by his defence counsel, his parents and even Norwich Union, his insurance company.

After Mason had been questioned, the foreman of the jury raised a query with the judge, writing it on a piece of paper. The judge then asked to be seen in the chambers by the jury about the contents of the note.

They were demanding to know the whereabouts of the driver and the passengers prior to the crash.

Whilst it may have seemed a relative point, the judge was obliged to advise them on points of law only including the rules of evidence. In this particular case, the jury weren't allowed to even think about where the three friends had been before the crash. Even if they had unwittingly heard where they had been, they would somehow have to expunge these facts from their minds before reaching a majority verdict. I was aware of all the facts, but the jury members, who should have known, were denied this very important information.

*

On the Friday morning, the jury were asked to consider all the admissible evidence before finally reaching their verdict. The jury's deliberation must have taken in excess of four hours.

Just after lunch, the judge asked them to return to the court-room and asked whether they had reached a satisfactory majority verdict. The foreman replied that they had.

Then came the moment I, and my family and friends, had been waiting for.

Guilty.

The foreman's announcement was accompanied by the usual drama and gasps of exasperation from the defendant's supporters. The judge announced that it was a 10 – 2 majority in our favour.

But, in a surprising deviation from usual court procedure, the judge did not ask for the jury to leave the courtroom when he handed down Mason's sentence.

I did not know at the time why he did this, but it soon became apparent as the judge wanted the jury to hear all of Mason's antecedents, including a number of previous driving convictions – one of which included drink-driving.

I couldn't help but look across at the jury to observe their reaction to Mason's appalling track record. It was soon evident which two had believed that Mason was innocent.

Both lady jurors were in shock as they covered their faces with their hands as they listened to the judge's recommendations as well as realising what a menace Mason had been on the roads even before he killed my son.

The judge recommended that Mason should serve two years in prison and also be banned from driving for five years. He also insisted that he be obliged to take an extended driving test before he sat behind the wheel of a car again.

It was registered in the coroner's court that Kevin Duggan died as a result of Paul Mason's dangerous driving.

Our campaign group was fully vindicated in ensuring that Mason had finally been made to answer for some very serious charges.

But whilst Mason had been subsequently convicted and sentenced, had his punishment fitted the crime?

It was now time for our campaign group to take on the lawmakers who in this particular case had almost failed to stop the lawbreaker.

Declan Duggan

Chapter Twelve

The guilty verdict from Luton Crown Court on 15th October 1999 gave me a real sense of relief, but perhaps oddly, no feeling of victory. Obviously, nothing could ever compensate for Kevin's loss but at least my friends and the members of the campaign group had the satisfaction of not having to accept anything less than the conviction of driver Mason.

In complete contrast, the reaction of Mason's family was understandably one of shock and distress, despite the jury delivering the correct verdict. Since I was the one mainly responsible for putting their son behind bars, I was now their public enemy number one and I guess they weren't going to let me forget that fact.

How ironic that I was the one being vilified by Paul Mason's family, even though I was the one who actually lost my son. My only regret from this case was that if I had anything to do with administration of justice then Philip Mason would also have joined his son in prison. To this day, I still hold him as much responsible for Kevin's death as I do his pampered son.

It didn't bother me personally whether or not the Masons showed me or my family any respect but it was their insensitive and irresponsible attitude during the aftermath of the tragedy, as well as their complete contempt of law and order and the sheer lack of justice, that I personally couldn't stomach.

I did not feel any sympathy for them, especially when I witnessed their reaction as their son was sent down, but again I didn't feel his conviction signified any kind of revenge for the profound loss I was still feeling for my son, 12 months after the tragedy.

The Mason family couldn't be expected to react in any other way in defence of their son, even if I did find their methods in attempting to secure his acquittal unpalatable. However, observing Paul Mason driving around in a brand new Ford Mondeo only days after being discharged from hospital, when he was supposed to be helping the police with their enquiries, was undoubtedly just as about as obscene as it got for me.

Obviously Mason's miraculous recovery from the crash and the carnage he had caused was being hailed as some kind of celebration by his family. What better way to celebrate their son coming out of hospital than to spoil him again with a similar vehicle, one of the most powerful sports edition models on the road? A warped way of thinking, most would agree.

Just like their treatment of a crippled Paul Anstey after they had coerced him into giving a false statement while in hospital, his dismissal from their company on the day he was discharged, was as inhumane as the treatment which I and my family have received right up to this day. The Masons' bitterness may have driven them apart but that is something I can't prove and needless to say, I am never prepared to forgive them for the pain their son has caused my family.

Likewise, Mason's insurance company, Norwich Union, have much to answer for in this particular case. The insurance broker, and personal friend, who accepted the late night telephone call from Philip Mason, approximately two hours after the crash, was fully aware of the appalling driving record of Paul Mason and the risk he posed to other drivers and pedestrians while driving on the roads.

Yet, despite being a convicted drink-driver, Mason was somehow being protected, even though he had only just served a 12 month driving ban.

To this day I cannot fathom why this was the first call a father would make on receiving news that his son had been involved in a fatal car crash.

The evidence in court also revealed that Mason also had two speeding offences and had been cautioned for overloading one of his father's vans. Philip Mason knew exactly what his son was like behind the wheel of a car and apparently so too did Norwich Union, but they all still contrived to leave a potential menace have the freedom of the highway.

It was hard to imagine how a multinational company like Norwich Union, along with Philip Mason, could conspire to give a convicted 19-year-old drink-driver the insurance to drive his Mondeo car on the night of the crash. It was very irresponsible for such an organisation not to feel in any way responsible for the carnage caused by such a tearaway driver, which was also hard for me to stomach.

I had considered taking out a private prosecution against both parties, but the general consensus of legal advice both I and Phil Maule had received, was to quit while we were ahead. We were actually warned that no one would take on a case such as ours due to the pressure that insurers would put on them.

The trial had been quite an ordeal for all of us. However, from a more positive point of view, 1999 was also perhaps one of the most enlightening and stimulating years of my life. It is quite likely for instance, I would never have discovered how the justice system worked were it not for my own personal tragedy.

But although I was far from elated that we had succeeded in securing a guilty verdict, I was both relieved and glad that the judicial system had worked even if it was more to do with the integrity of the impartial jury members rather than the complete co-operation of the police.

Despite that protracted battle with the local police service, who blatantly attempted to mislead me during those early stages of the investigation, my faith in the justice system had been temporarily restored but that was no consolation for the loss of Kevin's life.

Securing a guilty verdict may also have meant that the police could have been seen as somewhat discredited. That fact would have been a bitter pill for some of them to swallow and it could be argued that it is probably one of the reasons why I am still coming in for special attention by some of them to this very day!

My faith in humanity has been restored by that correct verdict, and although PC Whinnett and some of his colleagues offered me their congratulations, it was hard to believe whether or not there was real sincerity in their gesture.

The CPS and prosecution barrister, Amjad Malik, also congratulated and thanked the campaign group for their intelligence gathering work in the preparation of the case. The guilty verdict certainly gave me enormous comfort as part of my own grieving process, and I continue to believe that similar positive results would be far more constructive than any forms of revenge could ever achieve.

*

The general consensus amongst our small campaign group was that Mason's two year sentence simply didn't reflect the gravity of his crime.

It was now time to explore the possibility of what could be done to ensure that the jury in a similar case in the future would be able to hear all the facts and not be denied the results of a suspect drink-driver's blood test before reaching their verdict.

Two years imprisonment for the taking of a life still seemed too lenient a sentence to all of us in the group. Paul Mason actually only served nine months (somehow ironic when you think that it took nine months for Kevin to come into this world!) and that was something beyond our control.

Since we were not entirely satisfied with Mason's sentence, the least we could do was to ensure that no future victims of a similar irresponsible driver would have to endure the same kind of obstacles that we had to face in order to bring a suspect drink-driver to court.

The law at that time may have failed me but I was determined that future families in my situation wouldn't have to suffer the same kind of frustration with the existing laws on obtaining evidence from an unconscious drink-drive suspect.

The consent laws and infringement of human rights of a non-conscious drink-drive suspect was clearly a legal loophole that could have cost lives and needed to be amended immediately.

Although we were successful in getting a conviction of causing death by dangerous driving, the overall result still felt so hollow.

All of us involved in the investigation had learnt much from the trial and the procedures heading into the court case. We were therefore determined to make full use of that experience in achieving our next objective, changing the drink-drive law, namely the advent of what was to become known as 'Duggan's Law'.

Whilst our campaign group had been primarily involved in the preparation for the court case in October, much progress had also been made since Phil Maule and I visited Parliament in June to see Gwyneth Dunwoody MP.

In the immediate aftermath of the successful conviction, it was felt that one of our priorities was now to seek an improvement in the sentencing process because in our case we believed two years imprisonment didn't fit the crime.

Margaret Moran MP therefore decided that now might be an appropriate time to go back to her Home Minister colleague Charles Clarke MP and campaign for stiffer sentences for this particular type of crime.

My own feelings at that time were that Paul Mason was responsible for Kevin's manslaughter at the very least. Unfortunately because he used a car rather than a recognised weapon it appeared to lessen the impact or scale of the crime.

Achieving a change in law was far from straightforward, especially when it meant taking on the powerful UK Transport lobby which appears (then and now) to have considerable influence over policy-making decisions and the country's justice system. Death by vehicle rather than any other method also appeared to be treated as a special case in this country.

These sentiments were echoed by Gwyneth Dunwoody who once said in the House of Commons during a debate on this very subject that if one wanted to murder someone in this country and get away with it, all they needed to do was just run them over in a car!

Of course that may have sounded extreme but it was also true and nobody was more aware of the deficiencies in the current drink-drive legislation than the Chairman of the Transport Committee at that time.

The campaign group had an enormous hurdle to scale if we wanted to change the law. It would mean garnering support from as many relevant organisations as possible as well as enlisting the support of doctors and police officers, who would be the two agencies most affected by any possible change in legislation for blood sampling unconscious drink-drive suspects.

It would also be necessary to have the full support of the various government departments, not to mention all the relevant civil servants, if our campaign was to secure a speedy change in the law.

On paper it did look to be an awesome undertaking for our small group especially when certain leading civil servants showed no qualms in obstructing our progress.

But, we also did have a couple of very good civil servants who fully supported our campaign. I had actually never met some of these individuals but many wrote to me when they read about the campaign and had no hesitation in giving me guidance and advice.

Actually, any advice that meant an easy passage around government departmental procedures was always welcome and so their input was very important in assisting the achieving of our objectives.

The real ace in our campaign groups' pack was undoubtedly Margaret Moran MP. She did so much work in liaising between the various government departments which was vital if we were going to have any hope of fast-tracking new legislation through the various legislative processes.

Probably one of the best constituency politicians in the country since she entered Parliament, Margaret had a real insight into these departments and not surprisingly she also had many friends within them.

She was also a former private Parliamentary Secretary and close friend of the late Mo Mowlam[30], who was a former Northern Ireland Secretary and Cabinet Secretary and who had access to all department heads. Margaret was often able to call upon her assistance.

Mo was very well respected and loved dearly by those that knew her, in particular the Labour movement, as well as the Irish who lived in the UK.

In her work in the Government and on the Irish Peace Process she was prominent in obtaining the ceasefire in Northern Ireland and getting all the warring parties around the same table to work on a permanent peace in the Province. She worked tirelessly whilst also suffering from a terminal illness but she carried out her duties meticulously.

She was a real star and a gem in the crown of Labour party politics. She had a real connection with the 'working man' and in the grass roots of the Labour movement.

Margaret Moran invited Mo to Luton for International Woman's Day which was held on the 8th March 2000. The event was held in the Labour heartland of the Farley Hill Estate on the edge of town.

St. Margaret's Social Centre was to be the venue and was attended by invited guests, mainly Labour party workers and activists and many from the local Irish community.

Mo was in her element; she could feel the respect and the love for her in the main hall. Everyone there was trying to meet her personally and she didn't disappoint, making sure that she met everyone and chatted individually to whoever wanted to meet her. Mo liked to socialise and she also liked a drink. Not only did she like to let her hair down, she did at times take it off (her wig that is!).

There were no airs nor graces about her at all. Margaret arranged a quiet meeting for Mo and myself. We sat in the corner of the room and I spent about 20 minutes talking with her.

---

[30] Marjorie "Mo" Mowlam (18th September – 19th August 2005); Labour politician; MP for Redcar (1987 – 2001); Secretary of State for Northern Ireland (1997 – 1999); Minister for the Cabinet Office; Chancellor of the Duchy of Lancaster (1999 – 2001).

She knew of my predicament and was personally aware of what I was going through in the aftermath of Kevin's death. We spoke candidly and to the point, I brought up my situation of receiving death threats and poison pen letters.

She asked if I knew who was doing the dirty deeds and replied that I could only guess. I told her about the Freemason links that I was coming up against. She raised her eyebrows and said, "Listen to me carefully, Declan. The Freemasons have their tentacles in every walk of life. They project an image that they are this Christian, charitable, do-good organisation who have been given a hard time by some sections of the media and perceived as a certain type of sect."

She went on to say that although some of that was true, the Freemasons also have a dark side, with willing volunteers to commit dark acts.

Mo said she called them the 'Dark Forces', continuing that the police force and both national and local government was riddled with Freemasons and that many of them used these circles to promote themselves and fellow Freemasons in their own private and business dealings. This included the justice system and contracts that are handed out by local government officials.

She warned me that they were a formidable force and I should be very careful in what I say and do, because once they target you it can often mean the end. She finished by saying that these type of people hunt in packs or join secret societies because they haven't got the balls to stand on their own two feet and get on with their own life and business under their own steam, seemingly unable to operate on their own.

After that very sobering up discussion with Mo, we ended up having a great evening, lots of dancing, singing and certainly lots more drinking. It definitely wasn't like having a minister of the government at this social event; it was more like having an A list celebrity at a party.

Everyone who met her thanked her for being the straight up politician that she was. She didn't look like a politician; Mo looked and talked like one of us. It really was a strange, surreal evening. But I wouldn't have missed it for the world.

My mother and sister came over from Ireland especially to meet Mo. They really enjoyed her jovial company and she made a real fuss of them both.

As a family we decided to buy her a nice present that she would always remember. This was meant to be for all the good work that she had done for all the Irish people on both sides of the Irish Sea.

We commissioned a well-known local artist and portrait painter Peter Deighan to paint Mo from one of her many photographs. We let Margaret pick the picture and Peter duly painted the portrait.

The end result was a success and was a true likeness. My mother presented a gold framed painting and it was obvious to all that Mo was really taken aback and surprised at the gift. There was definitely a tear in her eye when she thanked us over and over again. We then continued the party until the early hours. Margaret told me some time later how Mo loved the portrait.

It wasn't until the next day and after clearing the hangover that I began to reflect on what Mo had said about the Freemasons and the 'Dark Forces'. I was still no clearer as to who was pulling the strings and giving the orders in an effort to put me off my quest for justice following Kevin's fatal car crash.

There were certain individuals out there in the world, formulating a strategy to frighten me off or discredit me one way or another. These people wanted me to go away and not to raise my head above the parapet and stop asking questions on the way justice and policing should be done.

Mo's words to me only inspired me to carry on regardless and challenge any obstacles that came my way. What was most chilling about the whole scenario was that the advice I was given was from one of the most senior members of the British Government.

Oh my God, what chance did I really have?????

*

I was frequently kept briefed on developments with the campaign and it was never too hard to detect Margaret's optimism about the encouraging progress of the campaign in attempting to bring about a change in the law of drink-driving.

The judiciary and a whole host of government departments including the Health department, the Home Office, the Road Safety commission and also the Department of Transport, would all be affected by any change in legislation. That was why it was so difficult in getting a Bill like this passed.

However, despite the legislative process being long and multidirectional, we were slowly but surely getting to where we wanted to be, beginning with our first meeting with probably one of the most pivotal politicians in government at the time.

Home Minister Charles Clarke MP could offer our campaign group positive and constructive assistance and so a meeting with him in the House of Commons was scheduled for July 2000.

Chapter Thirteen

A guilty verdict from the court case of 15th October 1999 was just the kind of impetus we needed in order to achieve the remaining objectives of closing the legal loophole on blood testing unconscious drink-drive suspects at the scene of a road crash, and also finding a permanent memorial for my son Kevin.

Much of the organisation for the second annual Kevin Duggan Golf Day, to be held on Thursday 13th August 2000, had already been planned but in the meantime the campaign group, represented by Margaret Moran MP, Phil Maule and I, also had an important date in July in Westminster to see Home Office Minister, Charles Clarke MP.

Unlike our previous visits to Parliament, this meeting took place at the Home Office in Whitehall, within walking distance from Parliament Square. On checking in through the security desk, we were escorted to the Minister's office, where he welcomed and invited us to sit around the table. Before getting down to business he offered us drinks and then opened the discussion by asking, "Right, who wants to start?"

Phil Maule took up his usual role of recording the meeting minutes while Margaret led the conversation with a short ten minute introduction before passing the 'baton' to me to continue.

Though I had described both the tragedy and the case on many previous occasions, I still found it quite stressful and nerve-wracking having to relive the whole story over again.

Unlike any previous perceptions I had of a grumpy cabinet minister, I found Charles Clarke to be extremely polite and understanding as well as firm and fair. I did my best to spell out my grievances, from the weaknesses of the judicial system and the present attitude to deaths on the road.

I also cited Gwyneth Dunwoody's concise analogy of the current imbalance between the rights of the perpetrator and victim when she said, "If you want to kill someone in this country and get away with it just run them over in a car because the investigation that will go into it will be virtually nil. After some administration and paperwork and with a bit of bad luck you might receive a court appearance with a fine, a short ban and some points on your licence."

It was plain to see that the law at that time did favour more the perpetrator than the victim of the crime. Charles Clarke listened intently and agreed that something needed to be done, no matter how difficult that might prove to be.

He was also impressed by the determination of the campaign group and what we had achieved to date, despite all the obstacles we had encountered.

Had we not been so insistent in securing Paul Mason's conviction instead of waiting for the police to come to us, then it is quite likely he would have evaded justice. I told the Minister I was not prepared to be treated like that again.

I also said I was determined to see this through to the end, whatever it took, and I wanted to know why such an investigation wasn't being conducted in a proper manner similar to death caused by train or aeroplane (as two examples), which would be followed by an inquiry.

Our stance was that death by motor vehicle shouldn't be treated any differently. It is incredible to think that 3,500 people are killed on our roads annually and are not given anything like the same priority as a train crash or plane disaster.

Finally, I pointed out how the case against Mason had been compromised due to the non-availability of his blood sample at the time of the crash and therefore, the court case resulted in a conviction for death by dangerous driving rather than manslaughter. Another example of where the perpetrator of the crime's rights appeared to supersede those of the victim.

Charles Clarke appeared totally engrossed by the case and had clear concerns about the gaping loophole with regards to consent for blood sampling. He asked me several questions about what I had told him before admitting that he never realised that this was how the present law stood.

As the Minister had agreed with much of what had been said, there was a real sense of hope in achieving a change to the law. He vowed to do his utmost to bring this change about. And although there were still a number of hurdles to be cleared, our visit to the Home Office was clearly the most defining moment in the whole campaign.

Supported superbly by Margaret Moran, there is no doubt that Charles Clarke can claim much of the credit for getting the required legislation in the Bill through the various legislative processes. His unstinting support eventually culminated in the Bill, known as Duggan's Law, passed in the House of Commons 10th July 2002, receiving Royal Assent on 17th October that same year. But that was someway in the future.

Equally, when we were leaving, Home Secretary David Blunkett approached us and said he was fully behind our campaign's goals and that Charles Clarke (as his 'number two') was keeping him fully appraised of the situation – he wished us the best of luck and wanted us to keep him updated.

Returning to Luton with the Minister's 'blueprint' for the necessary change in the drink-drive law, it was another moment to savour and celebrate for all our hard-working campaign group members in the White Swan that evening.

Two more years of tough campaign work lay ahead of us, but after the positive encouragement gained from our meeting at the Home Office, the momentum within the campaign group was now seemingly unstoppable.

Some of the invaluable advice we received included how best to make inroads to other relevant departments, how to lobby and how to make the right contacts. Many letters had to be written if the Bill was going to succeed in becoming law.

It was therefore so important to keep all the relevant parties on board. I can't emphasise enough just how much of a role Margaret Moran played during those two years. Despite being a busy Parliamentarian, she made a high number of personal sacrifices in her attempt to bolster the campaign group's efforts.

The importance also of Phil Maule as a recorder and minute taker, as well as the research ability of reporter Gill Harris, also played a massive part in us achieving our goals.

*

As the months passed it became increasingly clear that progress was being made at a surprisingly fast pace. Usually changes in the law can take well in excess of five to ten years or even longer, but that was certainly not the case with our campaign – we were extremely lucky.

The positive signals emanating from Margaret Moran MP, the Home Office and the Chancellor's Office meant that our pleas for a change in the law were being taken very seriously. I had to deal with regular correspondence from all the relevant parties and government departments. All this progress was most reassuring to our small campaign group.

On Phil Maule and my first (of a number) return visit to the House of Commons, I was also encouraged with the progress made by the various civil servants responsible for drafting the new legislation – the Police Reform Bill (or as Margaret Moran had dubbed it, the Duggan Bill). I played an important consultative role in drafting the new legislation and was constantly asked for my views on the various amendments.

I was very impressed with the assistance I received from these civil servants. I could now see they were determined to get a positive result even if they were still wary of potential legal pitfalls during the legislative process.

Amending British law is usually regarded as a minefield but the relevant specialists were in place to ensure that the process was going to be as smooth as possible. I'll admit I was quite humbled by what was happening but also privileged that an ordinary member of the public like me was now at the heart of such a significant change in the drink-drive law.

Deep down I had always felt that my persistence would pay off in the end. I used all my persuasive powers to emphasise why this amendment to the law would be in the interest to all road users and should take precedence over the supposed infringement of a suspect drink-driver's human rights.

Sadly many of the Transport lobby didn't agree with the amendment and were fierce opponents of any proposed alteration. However, both the British Medical Association (BMA) and the General Medical Council (GMC) were fully supportive of the change in law because a doctor could now take a blood samples without risking a prosecution for assault by not having consent of the driver. Prior to the amendment, doctors could have been sued for taking blood without consent.

Our visits to Parliament also involved meeting a number of representatives from the other relevant departments as well as Lord Falconer – the Lord Chancellor[31]. A real consensus was well on the way to being established and an amendment to the law now seemed inevitable – but the burning question was how long would it take?

Margaret Moran and I were asked for our views on the progress made as part of the consultation process, as were those organisations with a vested interest in a future change in the law including road safety groups (such as Road Peace, BRAKE, and Campaign Against Drink Driving[32]). However, it was individual cases such as ours that really highlighted the need for a serious change in the law in relation to blood testing unconscious drink-drive suspects.

Some drafts of the proposed change in legislation were then produced by the relevant government departments which I was then asked to view before offering any commentary. As soon as a final draft was agreed then we needed to decide the actual timetable or schedule required to have the new law implemented.

---

[31] Baron Falconer of Thoroton (born Charles Leslie Falconer; 19th November 1951 -); Labour politician; former Lord Chancellor and first Secretary of State for Constitutional Affairs; Secretary of State for Justice.
[32] Please see Appendix.

It didn't go all our way however, and we had to compromise on the results of any blood test taken by a doctor, nurse or paramedic from an unconscious driver at the scene of a crash could not be tested until that driver had regained consciousness. Retrospective consent would still be required by the driver before the results could be disclosed.

If a drink-drive suspect then refused permission for the blood sample to be tested then it would be treated in a similar way as a refusal to accept a breathalyser test. The refusal to co-operate would therefore be deemed as an admission of guilt.

Naturally, I wasn't too happy with the concession but I had little choice other than to give my blessing because otherwise we would have reached stalemate and the amendment to the legislation wouldn't have been passed.

*

Following one of our most constructive meetings at Parliament, I could sense that the countdown to the new legislation was well underway. I was required to attend a number of meetings dealing with the necessary paperwork which lasted long hours. However, it was a personal sacrifice I was willing to make because I felt a real sense of satisfaction in being involved in a process that could eventually lead to a landmark ruling or change in legislation to the drink-driving law.

Whilst I already had the satisfaction of securing a conviction for death by dangerous driving, removing an important barrier that denied our campaign group a manslaughter conviction at the same trial was also immensely satisfying.

Little did I realise that when I found myself involved in the road safety campaign work, through circumstance rather than any personal crusade, that the Duggan name would be forever associated with such an important milestone in drink-drive legislation.

To this day I continue to be involved in the campaign mainly because of the regular correspondence I receive from other drink-drive victims and other road safety campaigners.

Whilst I don't pretend to be any kind of professional counsellor, I'm always happy to pass on the benefit of my own experiences to anybody who wishes to contact me. My advice, for what it's worth, includes the important caveat that getting justice can sometimes be a muddied puddle of frustration where one has just got to be patient in order to get the desired results.

Luckily, patience is something I've always had in abundance as well as being fortunate enough to have the support of so many great people who believed in me and our objectives. Equally my supporters are also blessed with a similar kind of patience for putting up with me for as long as they have done. It hasn't always been easy.

I have confided in quite a number of these friends and asked whether or not they thought my drink-drive campaign work had become an uncontrollable obsession of mine?

I was pleasantly surprised to hear that all agreed that my leadership of the group was paramount for its success and not just a very honourable and altruistic personal objective.

My real concern had always been that the loophole at that time needed to be closed in order to lessen the number of similar tragedies on our roads in the future.

A big lesson learnt from my own personal experience was, don't take NO for an answer, if you really believe in your objectives. Life needs not to be as bad as some people imagine.

It is possible to change things for the better if matters are tackled in the correct way. The real challenge is to find that way and being supported by the right people and probably most important – never giving up!

So many others in similar circumstances might have chosen to suffer in a dignified silence as they did not know who to turn to for help.

I was grateful for the opportunity of being part of changing the law which after all, was just another part of my grieving process.

Until I had first-hand experience of dealing with such a personal tragedy, I couldn't be sure how I would cope with the 'grieving process'. As I mentioned previously, everyone deals with grief in their own way, no two people are the same.

One particular example of this springs to mind how a friend reacted to the death of his 20-year-old son in circumstances unknown to me. This man insisted that his son's name was never mentioned again and he also banished all photographs of him from his house.

To many this may seem strange and perhaps even bizarre behaviour, but that was how he attempted to cope with his loss. I presume that same man also felt like me in the aftermath of the tragedy; everything seemed to be alien to him and so presumably he was convinced that things could never be the same again.

I can't explain how or why I reacted the way I did following Kevin's death, but certainly things didn't seem natural to me. Nevertheless, I tried to remain positive and refused to be bitter – I wouldn't let grief beat me.

Following that disastrous meeting with Lord Whitty in January 1999, I could have become defeatist, but I stubbornly refused to do so. Without a doubt, they were tough times for all of us, but we all remained focused and then finally after two years of unstinting dedication, all of us in the campaign group were rewarded for our hard work when the news came through that the Police Reform Bill (Duggan's Law) was set to enter the statue books in October 2002.

And how appropriate that it should be the lady who played such an instrumental part in this truly wonderful achievement, namely Margaret Moran MP, at the official opening of the first phase of The Kevin Duggan Golf Academy in Stockwood Park on Thursday 11th July 2002, who delivered this amazing news.

Chapter Fourteen

Sport was an integral part of Kevin's short life and particularly his love of golf. After football, it was his second sport and he certainly had the capability to become a very accomplished golfer.

The establishment of The Kevin Duggan Golf Academy at Stockwood Park, Luton is undoubtedly a very fitting legacy of my son's untimely death. Not only is it a unique sporting facility but it also provides a very worthwhile community service to all aspiring young golfers who otherwise would be lost to the game.

On the second evening of Kevin's funeral, at the White Swan, the idea of having an appropriate lasting memorial was first suggested. A few of our friends were present, including Nigel Wright (who is now a co-director of The Kevin Duggan Golf Academy) along with Seamus McAuley, Johnny Edwards, Royston Wells, Marco Armitrano, John Clifford and my bothers, Vivion, Liam and Oliver.

We all had some previous experience in organising golf days or fundraising events and thus not surprisingly, we discussed holding a golf day in Kevin's memory. Even amidst the trauma and sadness of the occasion, all of us insisted on focusing on the future and how best to deal with the tragedy of Kevin's death.

Everyone was unanimous that plans should be made to remember my son in the most appropriate way and we agreed that the way to do that was through the sport he loved.

Wednesday 13th August 1999 was set for the first annual Kevin Duggan Golf Day at Mentmore Golf and Country Club[33] near Leighton Buzzard. It also happened to be the date of what would have been his twentieth birthday.

As has been the case at every annual Kevin Duggan Golf Day since then (the final one was held in August 2011[34]), the event was

---

[33] More about the club can be found at http://www.mentmorecountryclub.co.uk/
[34] Final one for now – we hope to do more sometime in the future!

divided into two parts; breakfast followed by an early morning 'shotgun' start for the participating golfers (both male and female) on the splendidly landscaped Mentmore course, followed by a reception and fundraising barbeque at the White Swan later in the evening.

Since the idea of actually building a local golf academy hadn't yet been conceived, the proceeds of the first fundraising event (which was in excess of £25,000) were divided between three autistic children in order to send them and their families to a specialised clinic in Boston, USA, for specialist training with other autistic children.

The outstanding success of the inaugural Kevin Duggan Golf Day quickly led to the unanimous decision to organise a follow-up event, which was programmed for August 2000. This was also unbelievably successful and several more local good causes benefited. Our small organising committee decided to review future events and what was needed for the event to realise its full potential, as it had now become a very successful social occasion in the Dunstable community. It was felt that the time was right to look at the possibility of establishing a more permanent and lasting memorial to Kevin.

Originally we did investigate the possibility of teaming up with a local football club but since our funds were derived from golf, it was only logical that should be the sport that we based our efforts around.

It was three or four days after the third annual Kevin Duggan Golf Day when the idea of a local golf academy in either Luton or Dunstable was first considered. I can't be certain who actually mentioned those words 'golf academy' but I do know that the idea came from the same group of friends and individuals who kicked off the annual Kevin Duggan Golf Days several years earlier.

The decision to promote golf to a younger generation of players was universally accepted by our sponsors and supporters. Our fundraising committee owed everything to golf and the establishing of a golf academy was our way of giving something back.

The location on the outskirts of Luton and also adjacent to the M1 appeared to be ideal. A number of years earlier I had noticed a small pocket of land lying idle which would have been ideal for a nine-hole course. The time had come to put the committee's idea into action and, along with Margaret Moran MP, we approached Luton Borough Council with the idea of establishing a local golf academy.

We met with the council's leader at that time, Cllr. Bill McKenzie and another local councillor, Terry Jenkins.

After a number of meetings over a 12 month period, the organising committee agreed to sign a deal to take control of the land, which also included Luton Rugby FC's third playing pitch.

Despite strong resistance from the club over the loss of their pitch, culminating in several fraught meetings, the council eventually backed the idea of the Academy. I remember attending one meeting – which I'd rather not go into in too much detail about other than to say there were all sorts of accusations being made about our alleged intentions. The resistance to the Academy from some quarters were very severe.

Nevertheless, Luton Borough Council acceded to our request to let us take control of two small sites. The area which occupied the rugby pitch was eventually transformed into part of the newly designed nine-hole golf course.

Phase One of the Golf Academy (namely the four driving range bays) was opened on 11th July 2002 by Sports Minister Richard Caborn MP[35] and Margaret Moran MP.

That particular day was easily one of the highlights of the campaign because on the eve of the official opening of the first phase of the Academy came the announcement of the successful passing through Parliament of Duggan's Law at approximately 10 p.m.

That was the surprise news that Margaret disclosed at the opening ceremony and not surprisingly her words were greeted by tumultuous applause from everyone present.

*

---

[35] Richard Caborn PC (6th October 1943 -); Labour politician; MP for Sheffield Central (1983 – 2010); Minster of Sport (2001 – 2007); Ambassador for England's 2018 World Cup Bid.

Apart from the excitement of the official opening of the Academy, I also had the added surprise of the unexpected glare of all the publicity as a result of the passing of the new legislation.

I woke up that morning to find TV reports about the new law, including pictures of both Kevin and myself. It was uncanny how the two events coincided with each other, and so we toasted the double celebration of the Academy alongside that of the advent of Duggan's Law (the new law didn't actually come into force until later that year, 17th October).

After the successful launch of the Academy's first phase, the next objective was to take the initial steps to get the new purpose-built nine-hole golf course under construction.

To do this, we enlisted the assistance of golf professional and friend, Danny Fitzsimmons. He had begun his career at Stockwood Park and played all around Europe before returning to Harpenden Common Golf Club, which was associated with well-known golf commentator, Ken Brown[36]. Besides being ex-PGA, a European Tour golfer and also ex-Ryder Cup player, as well as a prominent BBC commentator, Brown is also a distinguished golf course designer.

I was introduced to Ken through another friend of mine, Dave Matthews. After being told the story about how our idea of establishing the Academy had evolved, Ken was invited along to Stockwood Park Golf Centre; he needed very little persuasion in order to get involved with our ambitious project.

After admitting he was thrilled to be involved and after doing the initial marking out of the course, Ken suggested that it would be advisable to acquire the services of a reputable contractor to do the construction work on the course.

Before the tendering process got underway to select who the contractor might be, it was necessary to hire an architect. A Chester-based Scotsman, Ken Moodie[37], was hired to assist Ken in designing the

---

[36] Ken Brown (9th January 1957 -); former golfer; broadcaster and writer.
[37] More about Ken and his company can be found at http://www.creativegolfdesign.com/

course. His company, Creative Golf Design, which had also been responsible for a number of similar projects around Europe, then took full control of the design process. Along with Ken and myself, we drew up a shortlist of three companies whom we felt were worth interviewing as part of the contractor selection process.

Happily, all three contractors were very enthusiastic about the project but we all believed that the contractor most suitable were Contour Golf Ltd, based at Daventry – our dealings with them went through their CEO, Ingrid Eichler.

At the interview, Ingrid certainly sold her company well. We did point out, however, that whilst funding for the project was not yet fully in place (because it still had to be raised from our future fundraising events, along with the possibility of receiving Grant Aid, tentatively promised by Sports Minster Richard Caborn in July 2002), we all believed she was prepared to take a very special interest in our cause.

Contour Golf Ltd also had over a decade of experience in golf course construction, with work on three continents being completed with minimum fuss and maximum satisfaction, including Mount Juliet and Cork Golf Clubs in Ireland and Vale do Lobo in Portugal.

The company's reputation sounded ideal, particularly since it was supported by Eichler's own promise described in the company's website:

"When we look at a job it is with the eye of professional engineers and dedicated golfers. If you allow us to show you our previous work this will become apparent."

We did feel our prayers had been answered. Sadly, our dealings with the contractor appeared to be anything but the case.

Even though clearly stated in the interview that much of the project funding had yet to be raised, and although we delivered a substantial advance to get the project underway, our financial planning deviated considerably from that of Contour Golf's financial demands once the project started.

Within months of work starting, we faced a serious crisis. Because of Contour's limited company financing, the Academy simply didn't have sufficient funds raised in order to meet their invoice demands.

It was mental pressure I did not need. Although my professional advisers said that I had the option to walk away if the contractors were becoming unreasonable, I believed I had no choice but to tough it out. This was because I firmly believed in the project which bore my late son's name.

Thankfully, with the help of some of my great friends and family, we eventually got the course built and finally settled our account with the contractors satisfactorily.

I have no problem admitting that I had many anxious moments whilst the golf course was under construction as a result of attending many meetings with the council, my accountant and bank manager, in order to raise an overdraft to pay the contractor's invoices.

Members of my own family also stood by me with the offers of loans to alleviate my own personal financial plight, but thank heavens the news of the financial crisis never reached the local press. Without a doubt, I had many sleepless nights as a result of all the worries and stress at that time.

Sadly our relationship with Contour Golf Ltd never healed completely, despite the satisfactory settlement. While I am so proud of the actual end product, I cannot ever forget the harrowing times I experienced getting the golf course finished for the delayed official opening on 21st September 2004.

Although it wouldn't be fully operational until spring 2005, we decided to proceed with the launch of the new Academy in the presence of a host of local celebrities, including TV actor Kevin Whately, local pop idol Paul Young, former WBC world champion Billy Schwer, BBC football commentator Jonathan Pearce and Ken Brown.

The facility has enjoyed tremendous success since its opening. Not only is the Academy available to underprivileged children but it has also been used by local youth groups, junior members of the

Stockwood Park Golf Centre and the county youth team, but most important of all is that it has become a great family centre.

I'm lucky in the fact that I live nearby and therefore often have an opportunity to see who really benefits from the foresight and vision that our campaign committee came up with. It is also a great source of comfort for me to know that the course is also being very well maintained by the staff at the Golf Centre.

A year on from its full completion, and having finally paid off all the money that was owed, it was time to take the Academy to the next level. Because we were always so strapped for cash, we were unable to make progress as fast as we perhaps wanted.

But, we were always hopeful of being successful with our Grant Aid applications to the National Lottery, Sport England the Ryder Cup Committee.

Soon after the Ryder Cup, the Academy was visited by Ken Brown and Sandy Jones – both members of the PGA. Following a letter from their colleague, Dr PJ Weaver, we were all hopeful that the Academy could look forward to support from them sometime in the near future.

Then, 2007 got off with the best possible start with the news that we had been awarded with a grant of £72,000 from Sport England Lottery Fund. This was the first public funding we had received and was the perfect seal of approval for the members of The Kevin Duggan Golf Academy committee who had been so determined to deliver such a unique sporting facility for young people.

Later in the year, in June, Matt Green was appointed as the Academy's first Golf Development Manager. In association with Luton Active (who represent Luton Borough Leisure Services Department), the Academy began to deliver our unique golf tuition service to as many aspiring young players as possible, as well as introducing golf to young disabled and partially blind players. The Rt Hon David Blunkett MP[38],

---

[38] David Blunkett (6th June 1947-); Labour politician; representing Sheffield Brightside (1987 -); Secretary of State for Education and Employment (1997 – 2001); Home Secretary (2001 – 2004); Secretary of State for Work and Pensions (2005).

along with the CEO from the PGA, Sandy Jones, did the honours of re-launching the Academy with these new initiatives on 12th July 2007.

Subsequently, Sandy invited myself, Kevin Whately and Danny Fitzsimmons to Loch Lomond Golf Course in Scotland. We gladly accepted Sandy's kind invitation where we stayed at the beautiful stately home called Cameron House for two evenings. On the Saturday we played at a nearby golf course called the Carrick, where I played particularly well. However, the second day (after a particularly late night of heavy drinking and playing snooker!) when we walked the stunning Loch Lomond course, I didn't have a great game at all!

*

When we set out to achieve our dream of building a unique golf academy, we always felt that it was an onerous task. It certainly was that, but for all the problems and heartaches, I will forever be delighted by the end result and I'm sure that Kevin would give his approval with a firm thumbs up.

Chapter Fifteen

The most satisfying aspect of our fundraising campaigns is that they are entirely community-based. So many local figures, from every walk of life, some well known, others not, have always shown a real willingness to get involved.

I was also quite fortunate in owning such a well established pub like the White Swan. During my time there, the pub blossomed as a community fundraising centre almost from the day I took over the tenancy there on 18th May 1989 (my daughter Roisin's first birthday). From time to time I was approached by various charitable organisations from the early days to get involved in causes both locally and nationally.

One of the first events I remember organising was for the purpose of raising funds to purchase a Jumbulance (i.e. a disabled people carrier). The idea was to take sick people and invalids to Lourdes. At least £5,000 was raised for this organisation.

The NSPCC and the Save The Children Fund were two of the White Swan's chosen charities. This was how I met the then chair of Save The Children, Kate Robbins.

The first major golf day at the White Swan was in the early nineties in aid of the Rwanda Genocide. We raised approximately £3,500 for that particular appeal (CAFOD). Up to 80 golfers took to the greens of Batchwood Hall near St Albans before returning to the White Swan for the presentation that evening.

I was able to call on almost ten years of fundraising experience by the time of the first annual Kevin Duggan Golf Day in 1999. From then until the final one in 2011, all have been tremendously successful and thus, it is very difficult to single out any particular year for special mention.

Like so many successful national events, much depends on the inaugural one and for that reason I must pay tribute to all those who attended and got involved in any way. Over 150 golfers took to the lush greens of Mentmore Golf and Country Club on the morning of 13th August – the day of the eclipse.

Later that evening many of them joined their partners and White Swan regulars back in Dunstable for an outdoor party and charity auction behind the pub. I was staggered by the response to the event and that so many people wanted to be part of The Kevin Duggan Golf Day experience. It was the greatest possible endorsement that our campaign team could have received for our work.

After the resounding success of that first Kevin Duggan Golf Day, the committee decided to retain the same formula of organising the golf at Mentmore in the morning, followed by an outdoor barbeque party and charity auction in the evening at the White Swan.

That particular day exceed all expectations (even beyond my wildest dreams) when the staggering sum of £45,000 was raised. Victims Support, who offered me so much invaluable help and support following Kevin's death, and LUBYA (Luton and Bedfordshire Youth Association) were the beneficiaries on this particular occasion.

I am also a vice-president of LUBYA and have known their organisers (Colin and Catherine Ball) for a number for years, as well as Jim Marshall (famous of course for the Marshall Amps, but who sadly died in early 2012), their patron.

Jim's generous sponsorship also helped make the day a tremendous success. We were also graced by the attendance of professional golfer Costantino Rocca that evening in the White Swan.

I felt quite humbled by the presence of such a great player who travelled from Woburn for the event where he was playing nearby. Costantino was very interested in finding out all about us and our aims, and having spent some time chatting to him I was able to tell him all about the Kevin Duggan Golf Day.

Among the other celebrities who attended was former boxing legend John Conteh. I had met him previously at Harpenden Common Golf Course with Danny Fitzsimmons. Danny was one of the individuals who helped to get the golf academy project under way and was quite friendly with Conteh.

At the third annual Kevin Duggan Golf Day, LUBYA patron Jim Marshall introduced me to the 'Clarke Brothers', Steve and Jimmy Clarke, a fabulous dancing duo. They had been living in England for many years and were famous for dancing in some of the big movies, including with Bob Hope and Bing Crosby in the film *Road To Morocco* as well as *The Day At The Races* by the Marx Brothers. They had also played at six World Variety Performances during the twenties, thirties and forties and appeared with Elvis Presley and Tom Jones.

Although down on the previous two years, the third annual Kevin Duggan Golf Day managed to raise over £20,000 – this was still a tremendous amount of money for such a community-based fundraising event.

It would be unfair to compare one year with another because although we adhered to the same successful format, much depended on a number of other factors including the type of weather on the day or whatever celebrities could attend or not. As anybody who has ever been involved in fundraising events will know, much depends on timing and luck and managing to persuade both wealthy and generous benefactors to attend.

I can't emphasise how much I owe to the White Swan Golf Society committee of Nigel Wright, Royston Wells, John Clifford and Lisa Pedder (our administrator) for their tremendous work in making the event such a success for over a decade.

However, there was a bigger array of people who frequently sponsored or supported the cause in some way, either by subscribing to play golf, donating raffle prizes or attending the golf evenings by spending money on auction items which were the main sources of the fundraising.

Again, there were numerous examples of people expressing their generosity, including local portrait artist Peter Deighan, with his impressive work raising an amazing amount of money at our record-breaking event in 2001.

Following the third event, the campaign group decided to diversify into other fundraising activities. I personally decided to approach another well-known local community figure and friend of mine, Brendan Sherry, who runs the Luton Irish Boxing Club.

It was another very successful evening with the proceeds shared between the Boxing Club and The Kevin Duggan Golf Academy. Fundraising was all the more satisfying when we believed we were both providing excellent value for money and giving people a great time. On that occasion, we raised £5,000.

A further function, which became a very important fundraising event, was the annual Winter Ball at the Cloisters Suite in Whipsnade Safari Park. The inaugural Ball was held in November 2001 and was also a resounding success, netting a further £10,000 for the Academy fund. All those that attended agreed it was an amazing night and was to become a regular event on the local social calendar scene for the next four years.

Local impressionist and star of *Dead Ringers*, Jon Culshaw, was someone I met through his support of the Winter Ball. At the time he was better known as a local radio broadcaster and perhaps wasn't as famous as he is now.

Because of Jon, Save The Children campaigner Kate Robbins started to attend the Winter Balls. Kate brought Jon along to the White Swan on a number of occasions and he often entertained the regulars with his trademark hilarious impressions.

At our fourth annual Winter Ball, actor Tim Healy and his charming wife Denise Welch attended. A distinguished TV actress as well as a regular contributor on popular lunchtime programme, *Loose Women*, Denise was the life and soul of the party and, along with Tim, one could not meet a nicer couple. Sadly, they are no longer together.

It was that evening that I discovered that Tim is a very fine singer after he joined his son Stan on stage. Stan's band had been entertaining us after dinner that evening at Whipsnade.

Further fundraising resulted in the organisation of two charity football matches at the home of Dunstable Town F.C., the same ground where George Best was once persuaded by manager Barry Fry to try out for our local team!

Two teams representing former players of Arsenal F.C. and Aston Villa F.C. played out a thrilling 2 – 2 draw on the first occasion and then Neil Rioch, accompanied by a number of Villa's famous 1981 European Cup winning side, took on an Arsenal celebrity XI on the other.

Among some of the other celebrities who have entertained us at the White Swan, as part of our fundraising efforts, was eighties cult hero Paul Young. Now a member of the Los Pacaminos Tex-Mex band, Paul has played on three occasions. More recently, Dunstable based tenor, Laurence Robinson, has also given our activities tremendous support.

*

Two months after the successful launch of the annual Kevin Duggan Golf Day, I was invited to attend the Luton Irish Golf Society's Annual Dinner Dance, held at St. Joseph's Club, Gardenia Avenue. It was just over a year since the tragedy and their captain Peter Doyle and vice-captain, Carl O'Reilly, were very supportive of our objectives.

The leading figure in Luton's Irish Forum was Mayo man Frank Horan, who had also invited both the local as well as the Irish press to cover the function. It was there that I met photojournalist from the Irish World, Larry Cooney, and I was presented with a cheque for £1,800 for the Kevin Duggan Golf Foundation.

As the fundraising activities began to further diversify, it meant more and more individuals could get involved at whatever level they could afford. Whether it was £1, £2 or £5 for raffle tickets, or a much more substantial sum for a charity auction item, all donations were very much appreciated.

The generosity of some people was overwhelming and we received some extraordinary gestures of help through the post. I remember on one particular occasion at the White Swan when a man driving a truck pulled up outside. He approached the bar and asked for me by name.

I happened to be sitting in the corner of the pub, out of the way, when he came over and asked who I was. He refused to disclose who he was but said he admired all the work that was being done in Kevin's memory and duly handed me an envelope that contained £1,000 in cash. With that he left, saying no more save his parting words: "Keep up the good work."

Because of my growing public profile in the local community after a number of TV appearances talking about the campaign, it was quite common for me to be stopped anywhere from the local shops to even on the street.

Once, I was in the Luton branch of Iceland when a man approached me. Although he somewhat resembled a football hooligan, I was pleasantly surprised when he asked me if I was the man involved in the golf project. When I replied yes, without hesitation he put his hand in his pocket and handed me £20!

As the publicity and media attention increased, and particularly because of the growing number of sporting and entertainment celebrities who were kindly lending their support, the annual golf day became quite a pivotal social community event in Dunstable.

Consequently, I was also being inundated with offers to attend numerous functions, including a number of pre-2004 General Election fringe party meetings on behalf of Margaret Moran MP.

Since I was now also beginning to do some of Margaret's canvassing work, I also became familiar with some of her more high-profile Labour party colleagues including Ministers, as well as former TGWU leader Bill Morris[39] and Dennis 'The Beast of Bolsover' Skinner[40].

[39] Baron Morris of Handsworth, OJ (born William Manuel Morris; 19th October 1938); former trade union leader; general secretary of the Transport and General Workers' Union (1992 – 2003).
[40] Dennis Skinner (11th February 1932 -); Labour politician; represented Bolsover (1970 -); Chairman of Labour Party (1988 – 1989); former National Executive Committee member.

One of the surprise guests at one particular Labour party election function was TV and stage actor, Kevin Whately.

I'm sure I don't need to elaborate that Kevin is a successful actor who has become a household name since his association with successful TV programmes such as *Auf Wiedersehen Pet*, *Inspector Morse* and more recently, *Lewis*. Since our initial meeting, Kevin has become one of our greatest supporters and I regard him as one of my most valued friends.

Although I had serious plans to wind up the Kevin Duggan Golf Day after eight very successful years, many of those who attended in August 2006 persuaded me to reconsider. Since I had both family and business commitments, I found it increasingly difficult to keep the momentum going in organising the days, year in, year out.

That was the same reason why we decided to suspend the annual Winter Ball for a few years. Similarly, the running of the Golf Academy had also dominated my life so the time was right to bring in someone else to assume the responsibility.

Being involved in the establishment of such a unique sports initiative such as the Academy has always given me tremendous personal satisfaction, but there did come the time when I had to think of domestic responsibilities. Being involved in all the fundraising and campaign work helped me to keep occupied whilst also doing something really worthwhile in Kevin's name but a point came when I had to consider all the other sacrifices I had made since November 1999.

But, much of the work was fun and that is the real lesson to be learnt by anyone undertaking a similar initiative.

We discovered that fundraising can be far more effective when it provides supporters and sponsors with a day (or night!) to remember rather than merely resorting to asking people to put their hands in their pockets to buy raffle tickets.

What was more important for the campaign members was that such gestures of generosity always provided them with an added determination and boost in morale to keep going in order to achieve our objectives in my Kevin's memory.

Chapter Sixteen

A successful campaign to change the drink-drive law was always guaranteed to generate media interest. Consequently, many national tabloids began to take more of an interest in the story following the passing of the Duggan's Law legislation, 10th July 2002.

Up until that unforgettable day, much of our campaign work to change the law as well as our fundraising work for the fledgling Golf Academy had remained a local story. One of the tabloids did take a special interest in us however: The Sun. Before the end of 2002, I found myself being nominated for an Oyster Award, of which The Sun was one of the leading sponsors.

I was nominated by a group of MPs and researchers in the House of Commons for my campaign work. The ceremony, which was hosted by the Camelot Group, The Sun and an organisation called Common Purpose, was held at London's Shakespeare's UnderGlobe Theatre, on Thursday 28th November 2002.

The highlight of this rare evening in London's West End was the presentation of seven awards in recognition of work undertaken in various categories – I was nominated in the category of Governance.

I attended the ceremony accompanied by my wife Derry and my daughters, Roisin and Kerrie. It was also quite appropriate that someone who had been at the heart of our campaign, Margaret Moran MP, also joined us later on for what was a glittering occasion.

Among the attendees was Cherie Blair[41] QC, a number of government ministers, including guest speaker and Home Secretary (at that time), David Blunkett MP. TV personality Fiona Bruce, David Yelland (then Editor of The Sun) and Camelot's representative, June Thompson, were also in attendance.

---

[41] Cherie Blair QC (23rd September 1954 -); barrister; married to former Prime Minister Tony Blair.

In circumstances not too dissimilar to an evening at the Academy Awards or the BAFTAs, I found the whole experience quite humbling especially when I heard my name read out, followed by a citation on why I was being considered for such a prestigious accolade.

I faced competition from Neil Herron, who was better known as one half of the 'Metric Martyrs' who had campaigned for the right to continue to use imperial measures. Even though I never contemplated how I would react if I was lucky enough to be selected the winner, Derry, Kerrie and Roisin were wildly excited about the strong possibility of my name being called again.

And it came as no great surprise when they jumped for joy when my name was eventually announced as the winner. All three of them were so proud of me you'd swear I'd just won an Oscar!

Really, it was a marvellous and enjoyable evening. A delighted Margaret Moran MP was not afraid to show her true feelings of real satisfaction as well as a sense of achievement at the end of what had proved to be a pivotal year in our campaign.

A number of amazing photographs were taken with some of the other award recipients and nominees throughout the evening. A truly remarkable year had ended on a high for me, a year which had seen both the advent of Duggan's Law and the opening of Phase One (the Driving Range Bays) of The Kevin Duggan Golf Academy.

More recently, my campaign work has been recognised by the Irish community here in Britain, when I was awarded one of the inaugural Pride of Ireland Awards, sponsored by the Irish Post, on 19th February 2006.

Along with six other recipients drawn from the Irish Community, including the then Lord Mayor of Brent, Cllr. Colm Moloney, all of us were recognised for our achievement throughout the country and invited to attend an awards ceremony held at the Paragon Hotel in Birmingham.

The event was second to none in terms of organisation. I have been privileged to attend some great events in recent years, but the cabaret and entertainment provided by the evening's compère, Bob Brolly, was absolutely fantastic.

I booked three tables for my supporters. Apart from my own family members, there were my two brothers, Jarlath and Vivion, as well as my great friend John Hughes (who had travelled from Clonakilty in West Cork especially for the occasion). Closer to home, some of my Birmingham based friends, namely Paul Burrell, Neil Rioch and Bernie Murphy, also joined us that evening.

Besides the event being another splendid occasion, it was also an opportunity for all of us to reflect on our considerable achievements made in Kevin's memory.

*

From time to time, I have also assisted in a number of other drink-drive initiatives, including giving talks to schoolchildren on the dangers of alcohol abuse.

The developing culture of binge drinking amongst many young people of Britain and Ireland has become quite alarming. In many ways Kevin was a victim of this irresponsible behaviour as much as the act of dangerous driving, why I am determined to continue to campaign against it.

Even though I sell alcohol for a living, I also believe I am a responsible businessman by ensuring that my customers will not be served if I, or any member of my staff, feel that they are not in full control of their senses. Sadly, this is not the case of many other publicans who blatantly encourage young people to drink to excess, irrespective of any of the consequences other than the sound of their own jingling tills.

I vehemently oppose any promotional campaigns for cheap drinks and I'm not going to maintain a dignified silence on the issue. While there is undoubted pressure placed on all members of the licensing trade to do exactly that, I'm not going to be drawn by big business into sweeping this very serious issue under the carpet.

Naturally, my opinion has not found universal favour amongst those big businesses, who seem happy to turn a blind eye to this irresponsible situation amongst some of the young people in our society.

Unfortunately certain representatives of big businesses and corporations feel no responsibility for some of the ills of modern society but in the case of binge drinking amongst young people, the problem certainly rests with the irresponsible drinks company who are literally fuelling the current situation.

I am happy to speak out against the current stance by some of the major brewers and tell it how it is, even if I have to suffer the consequences. I certainly believe I have felt the backlash due to my opinions, without a doubt.

In the 20 or so years I have been in the licensing trade, I have never once turned to alcohol promotion once as a means of tempting customers to frequent my pub. I am definitely proud of the reputation of the White Swan as a social and entertainment venue but I have never relied on this method to bring punters in.

My philosophy is simple: the consumption of alcohol is something that has to be taken seriously and responsibly. Alcohol in the hands of the wrong individual can be a lethal weapon and sadly the road statistics prove my point. As landlords and publicans, we should all feel responsible of our customers' welfare after leaving our premises and make sure that they don't cause all the subsequent chaos and mayhem, which the police and emergency services ultimately bear the brunt.

Not surprisingly, my forthright views have found favour with a number of road safety campaigns and whilst I'm happy to speak out, my opinions have not been received with unanimous approval. Nevertheless, I am quite prepared to suffer the consequences which are still happening to me to this very day.

My campaign work has included honouring requests to attend functions and dinners to heighten the profile of the problem of binge drinking that is so evident in our society.

I have also received invitations to speak at a number of local schools highlighting the potential dangers of the effects of alcoholic drinks on teenagers. Those visits also include bringing along samples of some of the 'alcopops' products in order to demonstrate the dangers and glean feedback from the pupils.

In the course of these school visits, I also pass on the benefit of some research I carried out into the long-term effect of alcohol abuse on young people and how it can wreck so many lives.

Sadly the campaign against binge drinking amongst the youth of our country and changing the attitudes of both young women and men about the dangers of alcohol abuse looks set to be a very long fight.

It does appear that the Government still appears to lack the imagination to tackle the problem other than proposals to levy higher taxes on alcohol. I personally don't agree with the idea that a few extra pence on a drink will make a significant difference to the problem. Serious debate and consultation is what is really required, as well as taking some very tough decisions.

Until parents begin to demonstrate a better example to their children and accept more responsibility for their behaviour, attitudes towards alcohol abuse are unlikely to change.

Furthermore, making alcohol available as cheaply as possible from the producers who package it, before finally passing it onto supermarkets and pub chains who sell it to our customers is just one of the problem areas that needs to be addressed sooner rather than later.

Also, the easy availability of alcohol is a huge problem for today's society. The shelves of all our leading supermarkets are stacked with cheap alcohol, which is another reason why young and underage drinkers are vulnerable to the temptation of alcohol abuse. Some of the bigger supermarkets are selling bottles of strong Belgian lager for less than a can of Coke!

To me, it's so obvious that this is the real problem but also where the responsibility lies.

But, for whatever reason, governments are not targeting this problem. Although the excise on alcohol is a considerable part of the government's exchequer, cheap alcohol should still not be used as a 'loss leader' in order to attract customers into a supermarket.

The press could also be more constructive and responsible in their reporting on the dangers of binge drinking and its effects on society. While the practice of antisocial behaviour always appears to be capturing the headlines, it would be much better if the plight of some individuals, as a result of drink and drugs, was highlighted.

Likewise, high-profile individuals and celebrities who manage to evade the consequences of breaking the law are always good for a headline.

Celebrity lawyer Nick Freeman, alias Mr Loophole, makes his living out of finding loopholes in the driving offences of some of his high profile clients.

Having found himself on the wrong end of the law in recent times, Freeman also got one of his lesser-known clients off a drink-drive charge in late 2006. Because of an irregularity on who actually took the blood sample from the unconscious drink-drive suspect, the presence of Duggan's Law proved ineffective on this occasion when a nurse's sample proved to be inadmissible in court because it should have been taken by a police surgeon.

My growing reputation as a road safety campaigner has meant that I'm in frequent demand to offer my support to various pressure groups. In May 2006, I was approached by the Casualty Reduction Partnership in south Bedfordshire to see if I would be prepared to get involved in one of their campaigns to reduce the number of car crashes on the road.

I spoke on this subject on Chiltern Radio and met up with a member of the road safety campaign group who was interested in meeting someone personally affected by a road crash fatality.

I was pleased to oblige and told my story; the radio producers were very satisfied with the result. The campaign ran for three or so months and I was more than happy to be involved and would do so again. It will never be possible to eradicate all road traffic offences but at least if drivers show more responsibility behind the wheel, then we should at least be able to look forward to far less recorded road incidents.

Cars and other road vehicles are becoming more powerful with every passing year, so it makes sense that drivers should have far better training before taking responsibility of them. I believe that all young qualified drivers between the ages of 17 and 21 should be put on a 12 month probation period after passing their test.

Shock treatment for younger drivers delivered through the medium of DVDs, showing the consequences of irresponsible bad and careless driving, might also be an effective deterrent.

Several other campaign groups who have sought my support include the Campaign Against Drink Driving (CADD), Road Peace and the Road Victims Trust. I have also been asked many times to give my views and opinions on road safety and crime reduction on our roads on TV and radio.

The Kevin Duggan Golf Academy has also received much deserved acclaim. The concept of the new Academy received a most prestigious award in December 2006. As part of the Golf Academy's recognition to the promotion of the sport, Golf Monthly magazine nominated it for an award just prior to Christmas 2006[42].

But perhaps the greatest endorsement this unique community-based sports facility has received was its award of a £72,000 UK Sports Lottery Grant in January 2007. It was well deserved.

---

[42] Which I subsequently won. It was called the "Golfer of Endeavour Award" and the prize was a five night golfing holiday in Masseria San Domenico, in Italy. My friend Tony Rudkin came with me.

Chapter Seventeen

Truth be told, probably the most depressing aspect over the past decade whilst conducting our campaign was the fact that there were certain individuals who didn't agree with our objectives. No matter what one does, or how honourable one's intentions are, it is inevitable somebody somewhere will be upset by what you do along the way.

It is quite likely that even writing my own account of the tragedy will have some negative consequences for me from my adversaries. There is also sadly the inevitability that amongst the many letters of goodwill and requests for help and advice that I receive daily, letters accusing me of attention-seeking and hypocrisy raise their ugly heads from time to time.

Within these pages I have deliberately avoided making any reference to the constant intervention and distractions of certain cowardly anonymous individuals who oppose and even condemn what I have achieved within the last decade.

I was well aware that I might have been capable of making enemies along the way for various reasons but I could never have imagined it might have become quite vitriolic as it did at times.

Taking on the police and exposing some of their deficiencies has certainly not endeared me to some members of the establishment. Because I am a publican, as well as a road safety campaigner, it has also been claimed to be a conflict of interest according to certain individuals, not to mention being singled out for special attention by members of the local constabulary and the licensing authorities.

In early 2006, my brother Vivion, who was deputising for me at the White Swan and had use of my car whilst I was away on holiday, became an innocent target of the local police force for not wearing a seat belt.

Investigating Officer, PC Tony Whinnett, had certainly not forgotten me or my road safety campaign work and presumably would have liked nothing better than to hand me a summons for a road traffic variation. A road safety campaigner caught driving without a seat belt would have made a nice local story!

Six months earlier, I found myself in conflict with the local environmental health officers, or 'entertainment police' as they are better known. As a successful publican and owner of one of the few family-owned hostelries in the area, I had an unblemished record with the entertainments licensing authorities and also the police licensing board, until then.

Despite being one of the best run pubs in the area, the licensing authorities constantly monitored the White Swan for any possible infringements of the law until they finally pounced in February 2005. I am proud of my reputation within the trade but that didn't appear to satisfy certain civil servants and local government officers who were intent on 'throwing the book' at me for a minor licensing infringement.

The 'entertainment police' left no stone unturned in their attempts to gather incriminating evidence against me.

At that time, the law permitted up to two performers to sing and play in any public arena without a music license. We were hosting a local talent showcase which ran for six weeks culminating in a grand final on the seventh week.

Each week, two acts would be selected from a programme of eight contestants. But, to make it clear, only one performer ever appeared on stage at any one time. Therefore, I was convinced I had adhered to the law in every possible way.

Sadly, the authorities thought differently and after many hours of legal consultation suddenly announced that I had infringed the entertainments regulation.

Although there were eight separate acts on stage that evening, in the eyes of the 'entertainment police', it constituted a stage of eight performers appearing collectively. In other words, it was one act with eight performers on stage simultaneously.

Without even as much as a caution, I received a summons in the post within weeks, on a charge of hosting an event without the appropriate license.

Suddenly from having a first class relationship with the authorities, I had now become Public Enemy Number One.

At a time of extremely high crime rates, including antisocial behaviour, drink and drug abuse, underage drinking (much of which is associated with the brewing industry), the South Bedfordshire District Council chose to target the White Swan because of an alleged breach of its entertainments license.

One has to question the local council's sense of priorities when those same resources could surely have been deployed more effectively elsewhere to maintain law and order throughout the community.

Despite experiencing some severe personal difficulties as well as having to deal with the pressure of ensuring the road safety campaign reached a successful conclusion, I was still very mindful of the fact that certain covert officers had my business under constant surveillance.

This kind of operation made life difficult for me. Why they picked on the White Swan rather than some of the less reputable hostelries in Dunstable can only mean that it was me that they had a problem with rather than the pub's clientele.

Eventually, after pursing me for a number of months, I was finally charged with organising an event without the appropriate music license in 2005.

Not even an offer of diplomacy through MPs and local councillors as well as the local licensed victualler's association could prevent me from being dragged through the courts just because of allegedly having one extra singer perform on stage.

I was found guilty of not observing a technical loophole and whilst paying for a barrister's opinion in appealing the decision, it was all to no avail. A last minute request for a postponement of the court case was also rejected.

After failing in my first court appearance, I fared no better with my appeal and was subsequently left with a bill in excess of £32,000 in legal costs and fines.

The outcome of the appeal appeared to be a fait accompli and I was left to ponder once more whether or not some faceless and sinister power had somehow intervened.

On returning from the Algarve in June 2006 during the week that the White Swan had undergone a complete refurbishment, I was beset with yet further problems from the local authorities.

The pub's makeover was almost complete by Friday 22nd June, a week ahead of a scheduled wedding reception. Two gentlemen entered the premises requesting to see me. They were actually 'plain clothes' court officers who had been despatched for the purpose of enforcing the settlement of an unpaid fine.

After being arrested, I was requested to accompany them to Luton police station. There I was put in a cell and asked to remove my footwear like a common criminal. The problem concerned a misunderstanding over the final payments of the £32,000 costs and fines. Apparently I had settled the costs element of the fine but not the actual fine itself (£4,000). I was given an ultimatum to either come up with the outstanding amount or I would be on my way to Bedford prison.

As it was a Friday afternoon, it took a little while for me to reach my solicitor. However, when we did make contact and he came to my rescue, he pointed out that I had actually paid the fine but not the full costs of which I was still within the permitted time limit.

It was a huge weight off my shoulders as I had been contemplating the unthinkable of spending the weekend in prison. I was quite alarmed however, to discover what extent these sinister individuals might reach in order to service their own agenda.

I was fortunate to have friends to enable me to get over this problem but not many small businesses would have been able to quickly raise that amount of money in a crisis. It was a clear case of some sinister forces out there attempting to cripple my business.

Around the same period I also had a visit from two bailiffs who threatened to disconnect the electricity supply to the White Swan if I didn't settle a bill for £20,000 there and then.

I admit I had been in dispute with my supplier for some time but I believed I was negotiating a favourable settlement until this incident arose. But I never realised it was that serious or even had any indication that the matter had reached that stage until the bailiffs arrived at my door demanding cash upfront. It was a completely unreasonable demand at such short notice.

Thankfully I was fortunate in being to call on the assistance of two close friends to raise the necessary payment of £25,000 (that was the amount owning, plus £5,000 security deposit). The payment had to be made into their account, in cash, that same day in order for me to be reconnected the following day. This inconvenience meant that the White Swan was closed for 24 hours. I informed my customers this was due to a power failure.

These were just two examples of the kind of harassment I could have done without but worse was to come in early 2006 when certain individuals attempted to undermine the credibility of my business by the use of 'black' propaganda.

Of course I can't claim to know everyone that steps foot in my pub but I certainly know who my real friends and best customers are. However, I was not prepared for the clandestine attacks on myself and my reputation.

I found it alarming to discover that some of my customers were suddenly defecting to other local pubs. It came to light that certain individuals were accusing me of poor management, including not clearing my pipes and the incorrect use of chemicals in the cleaning of the glasses.

I was actually unaware of these rumours for a number of weeks. My staff were, but didn't bring to my attention the fact that unknown individuals were maliciously misinforming and spreading rumours about the quality of my beer to my other customers.

It did certainly hurt me when I discovered that some of my friends and best customers could believe these rumours and decide to drink elsewhere. It was a bad time for me and quite shocking the way they were able to infiltrate my customer base in the way that they did.

I also received death threats. I received several anonymous late night telephone calls and at least six examples of hate mail.

The most serious of these attacks on my character occurred as we were preparing to celebrate New Year on the eve of the millennium.

The caller, who had a distinct Northern Ireland accent, spoke loudly and menacingly down the line but I refused to be intimidated. The dialogue became quite heated. On announcing that he claimed to be a member of the 'Red Hand Commandos', I retorted, "You must be with the Yellow-Bellied Brigade."

"What do you mean?" He asked.

In response, I said, "You are a yellow piece of shit and a coward who hasn't got the guts to face me. Only threaten me down a telephone line."

He immediately put the phone down.

I was quite stunned by this man's conduct claiming to be from a paramilitary organisation. In all my life, I've never had the reason to have any connection with any such group.

Yet again one has to question the real motive behind this telephone call and whether or not it had to do with any possible Freemason connection. Even more bizarre was the actual location of the caller. I later traced it to some village in deepest Kent!

While I refused to let the caller see that I was frightened in any way, deep down I was very concerned for my family's safety and welfare. When references were made (during the tirade) to me ending up like "your dead son", I had every reason to be concerned. Though, if truth be told, they were just faceless cowards who didn't have the guts to walk through my front door and speak to me face to face.

As I mentioned in previous chapters, both the powerful Transport lobby and the Brewing and Pub Cartel would also not have been impressed by some of my road safety campaign work as well as the irresponsible pub companies who marketed cheap alcohol to vulnerable drinkers over the past decade or so.

What did come as a shock though was the bad publicity the Golf Academy received in 2004 in some of the more right-wing press.

Under the headline of providing free golfing lesions to children of some political asylum seekers, a Conservative local councillor, Cllr. Viv Dunnington, did his best to rubbish and denigrate the work of The Kevin Duggan Golf Academy.

It was true that the Academy offered golf tuition to underprivileged children from every background whom otherwise would have been lost to the sport, but certain tabloid press put their own right-wing spin on what was really a community service for all.

I was once again under the spotlight and got an opportunity to speak in its defence and I was also supported by the then leader of Luton Borough Council, Cllr. Bill McKenzie.

Thankfully the bad press disappeared as quickly as it arrived. I was also relieved to receive an apology from the Daily Mail. Outspoken and opinionated columnist Richard Littlejohn also didn't mince his words at the time and a very disparaging cartoon was published about the Academy.

It certainly isn't a nice feeling when you realise you are under the microscope. Whether it is my business (in the form of harassment from the authorities – i.e. civil servants, local government officers, environmental health) or my family and I (via poison pen letters or late night calls), I still feel I am paying the price for justice.

Eventually I know all this pressure is sure to take its toll. I am aware that there is someone out there hell-bent on making life difficult for me.

I have sadly accepted the fact that there were people I did upset, and whoever these individuals choose to be collectively known as, it's beggars belief why taking revenge on an innocent law-abiding, decent publican will do anything to satisfy their agenda.

Nobody can deny that I haven't been through the mill. In fact I'm sure few will disagree when I say I've been to hell, purgatory, limbo and back again. There were times when it felt that I was close to the brink and even ruination.

Even if I am not unscathed after all my contrasting fortunes since Kevin's death, then I personally believe that I am certainly a much stronger person now.

My main priority must therefore be for me to return to living something resembling a normal life again with the comfort of my family and friends.

Chapter Eighteen

The idea for my pub, the White Swan, was conceived in 1988. I therefore decided to honour my 18th anniversary (or 'coming of age' milestone) with a special function on 18th May 2007.

Like so many previous social occasions, it was definitely a night to remember as well as being a grand reunion for those of us who had travelled to Jamaica to support Ireland in the Cricket World Cup held earlier that year.

Amongst the entertainers were The Duffs and Flying Feet, the Irish dancing troupe, who both performed brilliantly at the opening ceremony of that tournament while representing Ireland.

Our guest of honour on that evening was one of Ireland's cricketing heroes and man-of-the-match from their famous St. Patrick's Day victory over Pakistan in Kingston, Niall O'Brien. My youngest daughter, Roisin, also celebrated her 19th birthday that same evening.

Although I had dabbled in relief pub management on a few occasions when some of my friends and brothers had asked me to look after their businesses while on vacation, my introduction to the trade was purely circumstantial rather than intentional.

I am a qualified electrician which I practised after beginning my apprenticeship on leaving school at the age of 15. Although I initially worked with a local firm in Luton, I decided to go it alone quite successfully as a sub-contractor at the age of 21 until 1988.

Some members of my family had been involved in the pub business and I suppose it was really no surprise when what looked like a good investment opportunity presented itself that I decided to take it. My brothers had pubs and a club in Luton at that time, including the Sugar Loaf, the Butchers Arms, the Moulders Arms and the very popular Charlie Brown's Bistro Wine Bar and Nightclub where I was a relief manager from time to time.

The birth of the White Swan began with a telephone call from one of my brothers who informed me about the offer of a pub opportunity in the town where I was living at the time. Then known as the Dirty Duck, it was an establishment that had a poor reputation but in partnership with a friend at that time, Dave Synnott, we decided to try our hands at turning it around.

In the beginning my decision seemed like a crazy idea, so much so that after five or six months, Dave decided it wasn't the life for him. However, I toughed it out and, initially supported by owners the Inntrepreneur Pub Company group, I managed to make a success of it. The group were part of the Courage and Scottish & Newcastle brewery chain.

I was one of the first 'tied' landlords to be offered this so-called pub partnership. It looked like a very attractive package for anybody wanting to take that first step on the ladder in running their own pub, but, it is always the brewery whom come out winning no matter how hard the landlord worked.

I succeeded in running a very tight ship at the White Swan. Needless to say, the landlords of the pub company were never shy in coming forward and demanding a share of that success from their cut of the profit from the fruit machines to almost the shirt off your back (if you let them!).

Many other budding pub landlords were not as fortunate as I was. Since most of my family were steeped in the licensing trade, I was never short of support when the going got tough, which it did from time to time. Others didn't have that resource to fall back on and many simply went out of business.

Inntrepreneur eventually sold their interest in the business to Namura, the Japanese bank. Even though dealing with that particular company was anything but easy, especially when my lease came up for renewal, it was also the turning point that led me to realising every publican's dream – owning my own pub.

Despite all the unscrupulous methods they deployed, even intimidation, I refused to budge when they attempted to make me leave the White Swan and lease it to someone else. I was nobody's slave and certainly not to any greedy pub owner, whether they were a brewery or a Japanese bank.

I was given the stark choice of leaving the business I had created for a derisory sum or buy them out, 12 years after the concept of the White Swan was created. The matter had come to head with litigation looking the only serious option left open.

However, Namura didn't want it to reach court. As it was still the early days since Kevin's tragedy, I was feeling vulnerable but as the days progressed I was becoming quite battle-hardened and determined. I had more than one stand-up row with the Namura representatives and even chased them from the premises on one occasion telling them not to return unless they were prepared to make me a sensible offer.

Within a matter of days from a court appearance, they finally returned to make me a 'golden handshake' offer of £150,000 in return for the keys. I was very tempted to accept and was given a few hours to make a decision.

After given it some serious thought, I decided to decline their offer in return for my offer to buy the White Swan's freehold. They subsequently returned with a demand for both the freehold of the pub and also the large garden to the rear of the pub, which had become surplus to requirements. With the assistance of friend Marco Armitrano we did the sums on a possible deal, which Namura accepted subject to completion with 28 days.

This deal meant that we had to raise in excess of half a million pounds, but I knew the risk I was taking.

My first port of call was my own bank, Barclays, with whom I had an unblemished record for over 12 years. But, no matter how good a relationship one might have with their bank, asking for a loan of half a million pounds was always going to be difficult. I was half expecting to be refused so there was no surprise when they did decline my request.

From there I turned to my accountant, Graham Keeble, who advised me to speak to the NatWest Bank. After one meeting with the bank, we arranged a lunch date with the manager and explained the situation. We managed to convince him we had struck a good deal which was way below the true valuation of the business as a going concern.

Bearing in mind I was going through a bitter divorce as well as trying to cope with the loss of my son, the threat to my livelihood was the last thing I needed and I can scarcely believe how close we came to missing Namura bank's 28 day deadline.

My saviour was Gordon Moody, a very reasonable representative from the NatWest. He was a local man and quite familiar with the campaign group as well as all the charity work we did in the pub. He recommended that the NatWest lend me 70% of the required funds subject to the usual conditions. That meant I still had to find a further £90,000, but thanks to the help of some great friends such as Jim O'Connor (a Whitbread account manager) and my brothers Liam and Gerard, I managed to pull off the deal in the nick of time.

Even though I wasn't a customer before I made the loan request, NatWest ended up lending me half a million pounds which was quite extraordinary. I had no collateral, but they had faith in me and I was pleased to be able to subsequently repay that faith.

Becoming the owner instead of the leaseholder didn't really affect the way I ran the pub but I can honestly say that the advent of deregulation has changed the pub ownership/management landscape considerably since I came into the business. While it's been good for the brewers, it is certainly not the case with some of the landlords or tenants who continue to struggle to make a living.

Because the breweries (and pub companies) make it so difficult for their tenants and pub leaseholders to make a comfortable living, many pubs change management every two or three years.

Whatever it may appear on the other side of the counter, I can assure you that the perils of working in a pub can be quite severe at times. Thankfully, despite the fact that it is a much harder business now than it was 20 or 30 years ago I consider I have come through it pretty well. I accept however, I am one of the lucky ones.

Although my priority was to secure the freehold of the White Swan, the acquisition of the surplus land at the end of the pub's garden also proved to be a very welcome and surprise financial windfall for me.

Part of the general pub refurbishment after taking full ownership of the pub was to landscape the beer garden and build an outdoor stage, which allowed me to organise a series of successful outdoor barbeque-style summer events. I also erected a high fence on the pub's boundary wall.

On the other side of that wall I was able to apply for planning permission, which enabled me to build six properties over two to three years. As a result of another road traffic crash, I was also able to acquire premises adjacent to the pub, formerly known as Roy's Glass.

The owners of Roy's Glass, the Ginger Family, who had been in business in Dunstable for a number of years, decided to sell up on hearing the news of the tragic death of their son Richard in Spain, ironically in a road crash. The premises were ideally placed for me because it meant I had access to my land at the rear of the pub and so I could complete the building project at the end of the beer garden.

The planning application for the Swan gardens development was far from straight forward and probably wouldn't have succeeded had the land from Roy's Glass not become available.

I had to make two separate applications but after some initial resistance, I eventually succeeded.

Supported by my professional team of lawyers and architects, as well as some great advice from my local councillor plus just being in the right place at the right time, it was just the kind of luck I could never dare anticipate.

I am most indebted to the Ginger family for presenting me with such an unexpected investment opportunity. Having endured a similar kind of trauma with Kevin's death, I feel so much for the personal loss of their son Richard.

When the building project at the end of the White Swan was completed, I kept the house nearest to the pub. Since there would be an element of noise coming from the back garden, I decided to keep that house and rent it out to tenants. However, with the proceeds of the sale of the remaining five properties I found myself in a much more comfortable position, financially.

Looking back I can scarcely believe how close I came to losing my home and business and probably would have, had it not been for the conviction and determination that I had acquired by not being bullied by the previous owners, the Namura Bank.

How ironic also, that it took another family's tragedy to set me up comfortably after taking a considerable risk when I was forced to borrow heavily from the NatWest Bank just at the start of the millennium.

Chapter Nineteen

The memory of my late son Kevin will always hold a special place in my heart. However, my personal loss has been compensated to some extent by the fact that I have been fortunate in finding some real peace, happiness and contentment since the tragedy of 31st October 1998.

Being presented with two more beautiful children by my second wife Derry has certainly helped me enormously with my grieving process since that terrible night.

Meeting and marrying Derry, followed by the birth of our three children Patrick, Danny and Sinead, was akin to my own personal reinvention after the tremendous loss of my dear son. My marriage also played an integral part in the improvement to my quality of life.

Our wedding day on 29th August 1999 was one of great happiness for the both of us, but for me the day also had a certain amount of poignancy about it.

Derry and I put so much time and effort into the occasion in spite of my own personal pain at the time. Somehow I found the courage to put that pain aside on our special day, even though my persistent grief was killing me inside.

It would be unfair to even think of my youngest son Danny as being a straight replacement for Kevin; his birth certainly gave me a wonderful feeling with a new lease of life.

Coming into the world at such a sad time, Danny's birth felt like a heaven-sent gift for me. Danny was born on 28th September 2000, which was followed by the birth of our daughter Sinead on 23rd December 2003.

Such joyous occasions were quite simply the equivalent of injecting new vitality into me. My heart was overflowing with joy as I could once again look forward to rebuilding my life.

In keeping with so many other parent's observations of their children's behaviour and idiosyncrasies, I sometimes observe them to see if there is any resemblance of Kevin in any of them. Funnily enough, each day I see them (as well as my older children), I see him in all of them!

Sinead's birth felt even more as a gift from God, because at the age of 44 and with three sons and two daughters already, Danny's birth seemed to be an appropriate end to my fatherhood.

However, soon after Danny's birth, Derry admitted that she had always hoped to give birth to a daughter and thus we decided we would try one more time for a little girl.

Our prayers were answered in December 2003 when Derry gave me the best possible Christmas present, our baby daughter Sinead, to complete our family.

As I've written previously, grief certainly affects people in so many different ways. Some people cannot avoid showing their emotions whilst others do the complete opposite.

But, if there is one thing that I have learnt since 1998 it is that remaining positive and focused, however desperate the situation may appear at the time, will always be the best option.

I don't believe I will ever know when my own personal grieving process will end or indeed, if it will ever end. While the passage of time does help to ease some of the pain of my heartfelt loss, I would be quite an optimist if I believed that I would ever wake up one morning and feel that 1st November 1998 had never happened.

My grieving process has certainly been helped by the tremendous support I have received from my family and close friends. While it would have been easy to continually feel sorry for myself, I never believed this was the either appropriate or correct course of action, especially after discovering so soon after the crash that the police enquiries into the cause of the tragedy were far from satisfactory.

At that time I decided the best thing to be was proactive rather than just being reactive. I also discovered that I had leadership qualities that I didn't previously realise I had, which was probably the main reason why I was able to muster so much report so quickly.

I was no different to anyone else when it came to dealing with the terrible news of a tragedy.

The usual human reaction is to make oneself busy in order to divert one's attention away from the pain, and although I continue to remain mindful of the trauma of 1998, I can just about manage to keep those negative thoughts under control.

Blessed with two more beautiful children, along with the success of the campaigns to introduce both 'Duggan's Law' and the building of the Golf Academy in Kevin's name, has served me well in my own grieving process.

I could not possibly have wished for any more since 1998 and I sometimes have to pinch myself when I realise what has happened and what has been achieved since then.

Without a doubt, and on several fronts, it's been a life changing experience for me, but I hope my family, my great friends and all the people who matter to me, believe I am still the same person.

Along with all the trials and tribulations, those involved have also enjoyed some happier times, especially at the many fundraising events.

The 14 Golf Days, five Winter Balls, three Paul Young gigs at the White Swan, two charity football matches at the local football club and one boxing tournament, not to mention my own two awards for the campaign work, have also all been part and parcel of my personal grieving process.

These events have brought joy and happiness to our family, not to mention the comfort of knowing that so many people wanted to offer support in Kevin's memory.

I was delighted to lead such a great campaign team and I would do it all over again. My life now could not possibly be more fulfilled. I feel so fortunate in having the support of a strong family and many good friends throughout my darkest hours.

Sadly my association with my ex-wife Linda still remains negligible but that is a problem I have attempted to address and which has been more than compensated by the great relationship I continue to enjoy with my five children who have helped me so much throughout my grieving process.

There have, of course, been times when I am still reminded of what the pain of parental responsibility can be like.

I have a family to rear and not surprisingly I also experience all the usual domestic problems of any parent from time to time. One such incident I can still vividly recall involved my second daughter Roisin.

It was January 2004 when I received a telephone call from Roisin's secondary school in Queensbury. Her teacher informed me that she was unwell and requested that I came and collected her.

Having been summoned to pick her up in similar circumstances in the past, I didn't pay too much heed to how serious the problem might have been on this particular occasion.

After being directed to the medical room on arrival where Roisin was waiting, I will never forget the look on her ghostly white face. Roisin's teacher was also very concerned about my teenage daughter's condition.

I drove Roisin back home to the White Swan. She ran to the lavatory upstairs. I heard an enormous thud as she emerged adjacent to my office. To my abject horror, I found her sprawled upon the floor.

She had been knocked unconscious after banging her head in the fall. By now I was convinced that she was a very sick girl and felt completely helpless in not knowing what the cause of her illness was.

I didn't know which way to turn to as I ran downstairs to the bar but thank God, John Clifford (a Health and Safety Officer and First Aider) was there at the time.

John accompanied me back upstairs and knew exactly what do to and what position to place Roisin in and did all the necessary paramedic checks. He advised me to call the ambulance, which I did, and we then set about getting Roisin into a comfortable position in the lounge.

My daughter eventually regained consciousness before taking an even bigger fall, cracking open her forehead. To witness this before my very eyes made me cringe with pain.

Thankfully she was soon in the care of the ambulance crew who diagnosed that she was suffering from very serious internal and external bleeding. They then decided to transfer her immediately to the Accident and Emergency Department at Luton & Dunstable Hospital.

Despite the trauma I had suffered following Kevin's death, what was happening to Roisin was still hard to bear, particularly the long wait for her tests results. It seemed an eternity having to wait for advice from the doctors, coincidently who also included the Moroccan doctor who had helped deliver my daughter Sinead only the previous month.

Roisin's heavy blood loss, soaking through the bed sheets, was proving this was a major crisis. To his credit, the doctor remained calm and knew how to deal with the problem. Following an injection, the flow of blood eventually stopped.

That long, slow, wait at the hospital was easily the most horrendous few hours I had endured since Kevin's death. More than once I had seriously contemplated the possibility of facing up to the loss of another child.

Following a blood transfusion, Roisin soon began to recover as the attention now turned to what had actually caused the problem in the first place. I was told by the doctors that she was anaemic but I felt I was being kept in the dark about the real reason. Finally, the doctor informed me that my 15-year-old daughter would have to tell me herself.

I did have my own suspicions that she may have been in the very early stages of pregnancy and had suffered some form of miscarriage.

Thankfully Roisin had come through her ordeal without any serious long-term effects. Such a huge bolt out of the blue, however, was a stark reminder of how quickly circumstances can change when you least expect them.

Roisin has always been a gifted dancer. She joined the Sheila Coxhill School of Dancing in Dunstable at the tender age of three. We watched her progress with pride and pleasure. Sheila always said Roisin had the talent to be a ballerina. At the age of eight she was invited to attend the Royal Ballet School (RBS). She was accepted and became a Junior Associate (JA) at the prestigious home of English Ballet at Barons Court, which opened in 1947. It moved to London from its original home in Sadler's Wells.

Every Saturday morning for the next two years, we'd take the train into London. The ballet school had a wonderful atmosphere and Roisin's face lit up every time we entered the beautiful old building. She suited all the aspects and aspirations of any young ballerina. At the end of the two year term as a JA the dream had come true; she was invited to become a full time student at the world famous White Lodge Residential School for aspiring ballerinas. White Lodge is situated in Richmond Park London. It opened its doors in 1956.

The school programme combined general education alongside vocational ballet training. This was the break that all talented young ballet dancers are striving towards in their dream to hopefully become the new Darcey Bussell . You would have thought that this decision would have been a simple one, even a no-brainer as to whether Roisin should accept and attend one of the most sought-after school places that all gifted dancers only dream of.

However, this turned out to be one of the most difficult decisions that I as a father have had to make in my life. Roisin was only ten years old and was also still suffering from her own pain and grief with the loss of her loving and very close brother Kevin.

At this time, we as a family were all quite vulnerable and weakened in our disposition, which made this decision so hard to make. I had just lost a beautiful son and feeling as low as any parent could feel, and was faced with a decision that I didn't want to make. It would have meant sending off one of my two remaining daughters to a residential boarding school where very little contact would be made for weeks or months on end. I just couldn't imagine living without Roisin or having her around me. I felt she was too young and too vulnerable and it would have felt like losing another child. I was torn in what I should do.

I was also going through a very acrimonious divorce from Roisin's mother Linda. We were hardly on talking terms and it was very difficult to communicate, and so this decision was going to be difficult and delicate to embrace.

Our eldest daughter Kerrie (who was 21 at the time) was the unfortunate one who became a go-between and tried to help us all to come to a decision on young Roisin. I also went to see Roisin's ballet teacher Sheila and asked her opinion on what we should do on a decision which would affect Roisin's whole future.

Sheila was honest and frank; she said Roisin had earned her place and thus deserved to go, but she also explained that when these young gifted dancers attend such a high profile school such as the RBS, there are lots of conditions attached that are not always visible or even spoken about at the time of being accepted.

The school terms were long and very hard work. They had to fit in all the usual academic studies as well as a full programme of dance. More often than not, pupils worked late into the evening. So I thought if Roisin went, then we would only get to see her at weekends and half terms breaks.

Sheila put us straight and said that was not always the case and now she had entered the dance world in the ballet school, lots of events and programmes were held at weekends and the children were encouraged to stay at school and continue with their progress!

Even the half term breaks would eventually be used to do shows and concerts and they would often do tours on the school breaks. Sheila was quite explicit and said that once a child goes to the RBS, works hard and enjoys the experience, it's then the school that holds on to them and tries to encourage the children to stay at the school for longer periods than we had thought and had first been told.

Sheila finished up by saying that as the years go by, we would be lucky to see Roisin even at Christmas, as by that time the students are well and truly under the wing of the ballet school and so going home for the children was becoming an extraction from their progress and we would end up hardly seeing our child at all.

So having just lost a son in the most devastating way, we had to decide whether to lose a daughter to the Royal Ballet School, of course in a completely different way.

After listening to Sheila Coxhill and consulting with my ex-wife Linda (through our daughter Kerrie), my mind was made up: I couldn't lose another child.

Conversely, Linda was of the view that Roisin should go! We had no choice therefore but to ask our daughter herself. What a terrible dilemma for us to put on those young shoulders.

In the end, the three of us did all agree that now was not the right time for Roisin to go off to boarding school, especially while she was still grieving for her brother and her parents going through - in what might have seen to her - as a selfish divorce.

I often think back now as to whether we made the right decision, in what was effectively a game changer in Roisin's future prospects.

It still wrangles me as to whether that was the right decision to make, how different would Roisin's life be now if we made a different decision and said yes.

Only God knows the answer to that question. This may be one of the few regrets that I have had to live with and will do so forever.

*

Another joyous occasion, which I must mention, was that of my mother Lena's 85th birthday when we brought her over from Ireland in July 2001. A great time was had by all and whilst there were tears, there was also much laughter.

So not surprisingly, her sudden death in December 2006 had a profound effect on my life. I had just returned from a golfing trip abroad when my brother Martin, in Dublin, telephoned to say that our mother had been admitted to hospital. She was in her late eighties and I knew she had been to the hospital recently for a series of tests.

For whatever reason on this occasion, she was not well and we were advised to prepare for the worst. Unfortunately, while I was readying myself to travel to Dublin, I heard the sad news that she had passed away.

While I know everyone believes their own mother to be perfect, any woman who was responsible for rearing a family of 12 has to be an exceptional person, which indeed my mother was. Undoubtedly she was the backbone of our family who held everything (and everyone!) together.

On the outside she may have appeared tough and uncompromising at times but she was also a warm and compassionate human being who enjoyed a fit, healthy and predominately happy life.

Soon after coming to Luton, she had a close brush with death when she contracted tuberculosis which was quite common in the sixties. She will always be sorely missed by every member of our family and life has just not been the same since her death.

*

My association with Margaret Moran MP remained strong after the successful conclusion to the passing of the Duggan's Law legislation in 2002. My aptitude for campaign work also meant that I was very much involved in her campaign work on the run up to various General Elections, not to mention the odd invitation to Westminster to meet her and some Department of Transport Ministers.

I felt so indebted to her for all her support throughout the Duggan's Law campaign that I accepted her invitation to join her on the hustings ahead of the 2004 General Election. Part of my remit was to persuade friends of mine, who were former Conservative or Liberal Democratic Party voters, to change their allegiance because of Margaret's tremendous constituency and Parliamentary work.

My involvement in Margaret's election campaign included organising party rallies in various venues and pubs around Luton, including my brother's two pubs – the Sugar Loaf and Charlie Brown's.

Our work certainly appeared to have the desired effect because she was returned with another large majority.

After Labour's General Election victory, another member of Margaret Moran's election campaign, Lord Bill McKenzie, invited a number of us to the House of Lords for dinner.

Before eating, we were all taken on a short guided tour of the Lords by Margaret before joining Bill in the restaurant. Among Bill's guests was Kevin Whately, who had also campaigned tirelessly for the Labour Party.

That was quite a memorable occasion and after enjoying a splendid meal, we were once again escorted around both Houses of Westminster. We even risked taking some photographs and I remember sitting in Prime Minister Tony Blair's seat!

Although it is almost 15 years since the tragedy, many of my friends still compliment me on how well I have recovered, but deep down I know I am often masking my true feelings. It's difficult at times to explain how I have managed to cope so well following those terrible events.

Although the memory of taking that telephone call in the early hours of 1st November 1998 still comes back to haunt me, I feel I can now move on. It has been a gradual process but I have managed to get my strength and sanity back and, more importantly, finally able to get my family life back on track. It's true to say that my domestic responsibilities suffered enormously as a result of my heavy workload and campaign commitments.

As those years have passed, I have slowly been able to undertake my daily routines from running a successful pub to being a good parent, despite the void caused by Kevin's death. Needless to say I am also constantly reminded of the tragedy when I pass or visit the crash site on the Tring Road.

I frequently visit Kevin's grave in Dunstable cemetery, but I don't rely on these visits to communicate with him. I can do that any time, any place, anywhere. Yet it also goes without saying that 31st October has become a painful reminder of what happened that tragic night in 1998.

My younger sons Patrick and Danny sometimes ask me about the brother they never knew. I usually tell them some of the funnier and happier occasions that Kevin and I spent together.

As Patrick grew older he became far more aware and inquisitive about the circumstances that led to his Kevin's death. Despite never knowing him, I used to hear him crying sometimes about the loss of his unknown elder brother.

The aftermath of Kevin's death has certainly been an emotional roller-coaster ride for me, my family, my fabulous friends and supporters. It has been quite a journey of contrasting experiences but also some very happy times. Furthermore, I have always tried to conduct all our fundraising events in the best possible taste.

The course of that journey has not always been quite so predictable but I am happy in the knowledge that I wouldn't have wished for it to be any other way. There was only one road to take and it was one which I took with a heavy heart, but also a determination to get something done in the name of justice.

A combination of this determination and my own anger spurred me on and pushed me to the limit. It was that mindset and conviction that also helped my supporters and I achieve so much in such a short time.

It hasn't been all doom and gloom; we have had some great times along the way. However, the fact that it was all accomplished in Kevin's name has also given me much personal satisfaction.

I was also very conscious of not overdoing it at times or being constantly in my friends' faces about the subject. Generally speaking, I believe our campaign group carried it off at just the right level and the results can be judged by the tremendous support that I have enjoyed.

As I've said, I don't regard myself as superhuman or even ultra special. What has been achieved is just as much a tribute to my supporters who were always there for me to keep me going when times were tough.

Often when I felt low or depressed, when I needed a shoulder to lean on or a leg-up, I always felt I had the full backing of all my great friends. I cannot emphasise enough how much I owe to my friends and family for their support, strength and love since 1998.

But the time has now come to draw a line under that remarkable chapter in my life and reflect on what has been achieved.

I have had the satisfaction in doing what I had to do in Kevin's memory in the most positive way possible. Duggan's Law has become a welcome change in the drink-drive laws and hopefully it will be of benefit to many other people. Hopefully, not only will it deter drivers who attempt to flout the drink-drive laws, but more importantly it will also save lives.

The Government and road safety campaign groups are convinced that the new legislation will lead to more convictions. I am sure that it will and hopefully the day will come when I no longer receive so many letters from heartbroken and grieving parents.

I have always maintained that ever since Kevin's tragic death, a part of me died with him. This is why I have strived with such determination to keep his memory alive for as long as I possibly can.

I believe I have succeeded in doing so to a certain extent but also that I have chosen the right course to do so at all times.

Yes, you could say that I believe I have done all that was possible...

...IN THE NAME OF THE SON!!!!!

Road Safety Campaign Groups

Brake
Road safety charity which campaigns to reduce the number of road deaths and cares for road crash victims.
http://www.brake.org.uk/

Britain's Guild of Experienced Motorists
Road safety association run by drivers. It promotes experienced driver assessments, better eye testing for drivers and random breath testing.
http://www.motoringassist.com/

Campaign for Better Transport
Campaigning organisation promoting sustainable transport and alternatives to cars. The site has guides, information, case studies, and activists' briefings.
http://www.bettertransport.org.uk/

Driving Standards Agency
Government agency responsible for setting and upholding driving standards in the UK. Conducts driving tests and regulates driving instructors.
http://www.dft.gov.uk/dsa/

Institute of Advanced Motorists
Registered charity dedicated to raising driving and riding standards and reducing the number of collisions.
http://www.iam.org.uk/

Parliamentary Advisory Council for Transport Safety (PACTS)
Parliamentary group promoting transport safety legislation and advising Parliament on air, rail and road safety issues. The site has research documents on issues such as speed limits, speed cameras, and local transport plans.
http://www.pacts.org.uk/

Road Danger Reduction Forum
Forum of road safety officers from local authorities. It promotes transport policies which prioritise pedestrian safety.
http://rdrf.org.uk/

RoadPeace
RoadPeace is the independent national charity for road crash victims, providing practical information, emotional support and advocacy to those affected by road crashes, as well as campaigning for justice for road crash victims and for road danger reductions.
http://www.roadpeace.org/

RoadSafe
Partnership of government, industry and road safety professionals which aims to reduce deaths and injuries caused by road crashes and to promote safer driving.
http://www.roadsafe.com/

Road Safety GB (formerly LARSOA)
National road safety organisation that represents local authority Road Safety Officers (RSOs) across the UK. Its aim is to support them in fulfilling their statutory role.
http://roadsafetygb.org.uk/

Royal Society for the Prevention of Accidents (RoSPA)
The Royal Society for the Prevention of Accidents is a registered charity established over 80 years ago and aims to campaign for change, influence opinion, contribute to debate, educate and inform - for the good of all.
http://www.rospa.com/

Safe Routes to Schools
Project to educate young people about the benefits of walking and cycling to school and which organises schemes to enable them to do so. It is run by the sustainable transport charity Sustrans.
http://www.sustrans.org.uk/

Road Victims Trust
A registered charity offering support to victims of serious road collisions and their families, in the Bedfordshire and Hertfordshire area.
http://www.roadvictimstrust.org.uk/

Scottish Road Safety Campaign
Project funded by the Scottish Executive to promote and coordinate Scotland's road safety campaigns.
http://www.srsc.org.uk/

Think!
Government campaign to improve safety awareness on roads, and to reduce crashes. Runs an annual campaign to discourage drink-driving. THINK! is about saving lives. It campaigns all year round to get people to think more about road safety, whether you walk, drive or ride.
http://think.direct.gov.uk/

TyreSafe
Project set up by the tyre manufacturing industry to improve tyre safety awareness. It is a not-for-profit, non-commercial body funded by tyre manufacturers, re-treaders and UK tyre retailers.
http://www.tyresafe.org/

Vehicle & Operator Services Agency
Government agency responsible for the monitoring of vehicles safety and environmental impact once they are actually on the roads. It supervises MOTs and the equivalent for larger vehicles and investigates traffic collisions.
http://www.dft.gov.uk/vosa/

Young Transnet
Website helping children and young people get involved in transport issues and research. Run by safety charities and children's organisations, it promotes walking, cycling and using public transport.
http://www.youngtransnet.org.uk/